a
Black
Man
Thinking

a Black Man Thinking

VOLUME 1 RAISING CHILDREN

Maurice Arthur

A Black Man Thinking L.L.C.
Oak Park, Illinois

Published by A Black Man Thinking LLC
www.aBlackManThinking.com
209 S. Taylor Ave.
Oak Park, IL 60302

Publisher's Cataloging-in-Publication Data
Arthur, Maurice.

A black man thinking. Vol. 1, Raising children / Maurice Arthur. –
Oak Park, IL : Black Man Thinking LLC, 2007.

p. ; cm.
ISBN: 0-9788340-0-3
ISBN13: 978-0-9788340-0-5

1. Child rearing. 2. African American parents. 3. Parenting. I. Title.

HQ769.A78 2006
649/.1—dc22   2006932629

Project coordination by Jenkins Group, Inc • www.BookPublishing.com
Interior design by Michele DeFilippo
Cover design by Chris Rhoads

Printed in the United States of America
11 10 09 08 07 • 5 4 3 2 1

In memory of Isidor and Rehova Arthur

"*Knowledge can be communicated but not wisdom.*"

— *HERMAN HESSE*

"*When you teach your son, you teach your son's son.*"

— *THE TALMUD*

Contents

Foreword

Earlier this year, I had a conversation with Maurice Arthur about Tavis Smiley's *New York Times* best-selling book, *Covenant with Black America,* which attempts to help forge a post-civil rights movement agenda "to create a national plan of action to address the primary concerns of African Americans today." After reading the book, with its ten "covenant" areas of address and action, Maurice brought to my attention a startling insight. The extensive covenant document, a product of reflection from national leaders, barely touched upon family or parenting issues. What a glaring and telling omission, I thought. Since then, I have spoken and conversed in formal and informal settings, further exploring Maurice Arthur's cogent analysis. The omission of the state of the family and parenting in the covenant compilation speaks volumes.

All of this means that Maurice's point and this project on parenting is right on the cutting edge, and it addresses a great need in our society today. This book is absolutely on point in addressing family structuring, parenting skills and strategies.

We know that the commitment and skills of parents are the most important determinants of the outcome and achievement of children. There are exceptions, but the rule remains that good parents with good parenting skills have great probability of producing outstanding children.

That is why this book on parenting, written by a parent whose own family exemplifies the points and principles made in this book, is so valuable. Ultimately, as Maurice points out, the goodness of the parents is not measured by socio-economic class, but by skillful, spiritual transference of excellent character from one generation to another. All parents need to be encouraged that in spite of their own limitations, they can do it! They must do it! Their children are depending on them. The covenant that matters most for children is the vision and commitment of their parents to their well-being and development.

May what is shared on these pages inform and encourage parents in every community to fully engage life's most awesome assignment: parenting and preparing the next generation to serve God and the human family.

Dr. Marshall E. Hatch
Pastor
New Mount Pilgrim Missionary Baptist Church
Chicago, Illinois
July 2006

Acknowledgments

Many people have touched my life in such a positive way. In fact, it often seems to me that I've received great support from virtually everyone that I know. That's amazing!

It is impossible to include everyone here, but I want to give a big thanks to those who have blessed me with their joy, presence and thoughtfulness. My gratitude to the hundreds of other people who helped me gain valuable insight into parenting issues—and never even knew it.

Special gratitude to:

- The members of the Couples Club at West Point Baptist Church in Chicago, Illinois, of which my parents were members, who showed me what good parents could look like.

- Mrs. Minerva Bell, my Aunt Minnie, who always shined an intellectual light on any subject.

- The happy memory of my cousin, Gail.

- John Carr, David Wilkins, Lorinzo Jeffries, James Barrett, Duane Savage, Myrten Byrd, Dwight DeClouette, Andre McLaurin, Wayne Morgan, Arthur Matteotti and Warren Riley.

- Mrs. Bashyal, for my education on young children and the methods of Maria Montessori.

- One of the best mother-in-laws in the whole wide world, Ann Cousin.

- My cousins; Linda Burrus, Yvonne Womack and Dolores Hutchens.

- Gary and Betty Wiley, whose children Jenny and Kevin were the role models I used for my own children.

- Dave Milburn, for his time and effort in editing my manuscript.

- My brother, Byron Arthur and my sister, Regina King.

- My wife, Tybra, and our children, Trenton and Morgan, for living the life that is this book.

Preface

A Black Man Thinking (ABMT)—*Volume I: Raising Children* is a book about raising children. As a black man, I'm more interested in the raising of black children, but many of the issues hold true for all children. Most of the parenting issues are the same regardless of your race, creed or color. However, as a percentage, more black children live in poverty, are raised in single-parent homes, drop out of high school, and are caught up in the judicial system. It is clear, as black people, that we are confronted with childrearing issues that other ethnic groups don't have to deal with.

There are a ton of books on parenting, and a few good ones on raising black children. One of my many blessings in life is that I'm the product of not one, but two great parents. Most people are lucky if they have one great parent and I had two! Of course, I didn't realize it until I was raising children of my own.

Over the years, many parents have been successfully using the same framework that worked for my parents and for my wife and me. My vision of parenting is based on my personal experiences and the voices of those with whom I've come into contact. This book is intended to provide a practical approach for raising children.

A couple of years ago, while preparing for a motivational speech at the grammar school where I had graduated in 1969, I began to think about my own upbringing and what seemed to work in raising my children. I concluded that most of the strengths and skills that I possess as a parent are because of my *own* parents and the environment in which I was raised. Probably seventy-five to eighty percent of who I am and what I am today is because I'm the proud son of Rehova and Isidor Arthur. I'll take credit for the other twenty or twenty-five percent, but without that critical mass from my parents, I'd be virtually nothing. Maybe you've heard that parents aren't as important to their children as they think. I don't agree with the notion. Quite the opposite is true: Parents cannot overestimate the importance of their role in raising their children.

My concern is that many young parents are doing a poor job of parenting. The hope is to have more good parents than bad, and even if the parenting isn't great, that's probably alright, as long as it isn't bad. Bad parenting virtually destroys children.

In the last few years, I have often found myself discussing parenthood with friends and family. On one occasion, after a rather lengthy conversation on raising children, a friend asked me if I had ever considered writing a book on parenting, since he always found my comments insightful. Writing wasn't something I'd ever considered, so I dismissed the comment quickly. A few weeks later, another friend suggested that I write a book about my parenting experience. Again, I dismissed the thought until I decided to take my own advice. Many times when giving a motivational speech, I've told children that they should listen to positive comments that people say about them.

"Often people see things in you that you don't see in yourself," is a thought I regularly pass on to children. The same was true for me when it came to writing. Those comments from a few friends made me change how I looked at myself and gave me the strength to give writing a go.

Let's get a couple of things out of the way right now. Don't look for an excuse as to why you can't be a good parent. There are plenty of ways to justify why you're not doing what you're capable of doing. My father once said, "You can always find an excuse if you're looking for one, and it seems that people are always trying to make excuses about something—excuses about why something didn't happen, or an excuse for why it did." Don't make any more excuses about parenting your children.

For the purposes of this writing, let's list a few things that are unique to black parents. Let's consider these issues to be facts and not excuses.

Consider:

- The infant mortality rate for blacks is higher than for whites. Inadequate healthcare for blacks is a major contributor to the higher rate of black babies born with under-average birth weight and higher infant mortality rates.

- Blacks have lower test scores in school. There are many reasons for the lower scores in both reading and math, but one thing is for sure, it's not because of intellect.

Many black children who don't do well in school come from low-income homes. Many whites who don't do well in school also come from low-income homes. Black and white children with the same background have virtually the same test scores.

- Economic forces have caused a shift in the job market that has dramatically impacted blue-collar jobs. And of course, the loss of blue-collar jobs has dramatically affected blacks. Loss of employment and income impacts living conditions. When a black man or woman gets a job, they are more likely to get paid less for the same job than a white man or woman.

- The median income for black Americans is 38 percent less than that of white Americans.

- The percentage of black children living in poverty is more than twice the percentage of white children.

- The median net worth of black Americans is less than 15 percent of the median net worth of white Americans.

- Blacks make up only 12 percent of the United States population, but more than 39 percent of the prison population. Something clearly isn't right with our judicial system.

- Blacks have higher arrest and conviction rates than whites and serve longer prison sentences.

- Until recently, prison sentences for crack cocaine were 100 times more severe than the prison sentences for powder cocaine. Blacks represent more than 90 percent of those found guilty of crack cocaine crimes.

The *Statistical Abstract of the United States: 2006* is full of interesting facts, so go to the library and pick up a copy or check out their website, (*www.census.gov*) if you'd like more statistics on many of these issues and hundreds more.

While the media's portrayal of blacks has expanded, America continues to mislead the public in believing that the face of a criminal is a black man. The *Statistical Abstract* reveals that more whites were arrested than blacks in 90 percent of crimes, yet you'd never know it by watching television and reading your local newspaper.

The war on drugs systematically puts more blacks in prison as felons than whites. In fact, there are more black men in prisons than in college. It's much harder to get a job when you're a convicted felon. So not only are the jobs harder to come by, the wages are lower, the standard of living is lower, and the hits just keep on coming.

These are just a few of the facts about black America today, so let's just consider them as facts, and say no to excuses. These facts don't have to make you, or anyone else a bad parent. Quite the contrary, one can still be a good parent in spite of these issues. We can't afford to wait for society to fix the problems it has created. We need the issues fixed and should press politicians to pass laws to address poverty and racial injustice now. But we cannot afford to wait for the fix, for children's lives lie in the balance. Take responsibility now for raising your child to the best of your ability.

Take responsibility to influence what you can influence and control what you can control. When it comes to raising your child, many things are within your control, and a great deal of others you can influence. You have to make the choice, but let's make one thing clear: If you choose not to be responsible, it is still a choice. There should be no excuses when it comes to being a good parent. You can break a cycle of low income, low education and the bigotry of low expectations.

ABMT is my attempt to touch more people in order to make a difference in raising children—particularly black children. There are many aspects of raising a child that are not included in ABMT, and that's no accident. You could write an entire set of encyclopedias on parenting and still not include everything. ABMT is intended to provide you with a different way to look at parenting and, hopefully, to provide you with some information that you can use to take action on becoming a better parent.

Nothing in this book is rocket science, and there is nothing in this book that you cannot do if you really want to make a change. A parenting handbook is always evolving, and yesterday's handbook may not have the answer for tomorrow's problem. All we can do is strive to get better, become a little smarter and be the best parents we can be.

ABMT is the opinion of one black man, based on my upbringing, experiences, readings, seminars, and the experiences of many others. If you find anything in this book that enhances your views on parenting or the lives of any children that you touch, then my initial exercise in writing will not have been in vain.

1

A Vision

John Richardson was excited as he looked out over Lake Michigan from his twentieth-floor Chicago apartment. John had made partner at his law firm after seven tough years as an associate, and Johnny—or J.R., as he was known to his buddies—felt that he had "finally made it." With a lovely wife and a two-year-old son, J.R. knew that he was truly blessed and began to ponder how things turned out this way.

Standing next to J.R. was Ricky Hamilton. Ricky couldn't believe the great views of the Chicago skyline, Grant Park, the Adler Planetarium and Lake Shore Drive. Chicago has one of the most scenic skylines in the world. In high school, Ricky had visited New York City and thought New York had a nice skyline, but he liked Chicago's better. While in Chicago, with its parks running next to the lake for miles in each direction, one could appreciate the Chicago skyline from many different vantage points.

When Ricky and J.R. were growing up, the land where they were standing was totally undeveloped. Looking north from the balcony, they could see the softball diamonds where Ricky once broke a couple of fingers trying to catch a 16-inch softball. A Clincher, the official 16-inch softball in Chicago, had broken and dislocated many fingers, since 16-inch softball is played without a baseball glove.

The Early Years

Growing up on the south side of Chicago, many of J.R.'s neighborhood friends never made it out of the neighborhood. Ricky and J.R. were best friends for the first thirteen years of their lives and did almost everything together. When you're the same age and live next door to each other, it's easy to become best friends. There wasn't a time that J.R. could remember when he wasn't hanging out with Ricky. Until high school, that is.

On their first day of kindergarten, J.R. and Ricky walked to school together with Ricky's mom. Both of J.R.'s parents had to work on the first day of school and Ricky's mother worked part-time in the afternoon, so she was available. From that first day of school until their eighth grade graduation, Ricky and J.R. were almost always together. While attending different high schools, they remained good friends and J.R.'s dad took them both to get their driver's licenses. It was always J.R. and Ricky, or Ricky and J.R. The two were virtually inseparable.

The Path Less Traveled

As J.R. watched the sailboats on Lake Michigan, he knew that his path was the one less traveled out of the low-income, poverty-stricken neighborhood where he was raised. Other than Ricky, he had lost track of all his boyhood friends. Since J.R.'s mom still lived in the same house where he grew up, he knew that many of the surrounding houses had been demolished and those old friends were nowhere to be found.

Before today, J.R. hadn't seen Ricky in years. Ricky left Chicago seven years ago and moved to Minnesota with his youngest son's mother. At the time, Minnesota gave more living assistance to unmarried women on welfare than Illinois. With her other three children, Ricky found that his girlfriend would get more money by moving to Minnesota. A few of Ricky's friends had already made the trek, and the financial benefits far outweighed the cost of moving. But Ricky had to move out of the apartment where he had lived with his girlfriend when the state of Minnesota found out. Otherwise, the state would have cut off some of the money his girlfriend received each month. Ricky still lived in Minnesota, since he had found a job working as a bus driver for a local school district.

Every Memorial Day weekend, Ricky came back to Chicago to check on his mother. He was excited when she told him J.R. had recently stopped by so she could meet his son, John Alexander Richardson, Jr., and let her know he had finally made partner at his law firm. Ricky called J.R. the same day he got back in town and J.R. had invited him over to his place. Not only had J.R. made partner at his law firm, but he had moved into a real nice condominium in downtown Chicago.

Work Hard and Treat People Right

As J.R. leaned over the balcony, he realized that he had never dreamed of his current lifestyle. He had only done "what he was supposed to do." J.R. did what his parents told him he should do. What do you do after graduating from eighth grade? You go to high school. What do you do after high school? You go to college. J.R. had never thought of doing anything else. He never had a "vision" while growing up, and knew that obeying his parents seemed to be the only thing to do. While J.R. didn't have a vision, that didn't mean he wasn't on a path. It just wasn't the path that J.R. determined, and it certainly wasn't his own vision. The path was the one that J.R.'s parents had determined, so it was very much their vision!

Standing on the balcony, J.R. felt a little embarrassed by his success. He didn't want his friend to feel uncomfortable. But Ricky seemed proud of J.R.'s rise to the top. There were no hard feelings.

"Man, I never dreamed of living in a place like this. Did you ever dream that you'd live in a place like this?" Ricky yelled.

Ricky's loud voice carried throughout J.R.'s apartment and reminded him of one of the many ways he and Ricky fondly communicated.

"Did you ever dream you would live in a place like this?" Ricky hollered again.

"Nope, never did," was J.R.'s response. "I dreamed that I would be happy, and that happiness might not look like this apartment."

"Sure is easier to say when you live in an apartment like this," Ricky said.

"Ricky, you've known me long enough to know that my happiness, our happiness and fun growing up, was never based on materialistic things," J.R. said. "We all were $.06 away from a nickel and it didn't matter. You know my mom always said that if I worked hard and treated people in the way I'd want to be treated, that everything would turn out alright. That's all I did, and things seem to be turning out right."

Two Boys, Two Very Different Lives

After having a couple of drinks from J.R.'s well-stocked bar, the single malt scotch had made Ricky more reflective than usual.

"You wouldn't think that two people from the same neighborhood and the same grammar school could turn out so differently," Ricky said.

Ricky was as smart and as personable as J.R., and in high school most of the girls thought he was better looking. But Ricky always seemed to get in a little more trouble. A little more trouble in grammar school led to a little more trouble in high school. This led to a year of college before dropping out. While college wasn't for everyone, it sure seemed to Ricky that it helped one's chances of earning a good living.

After one year of college, job prospects were not plentiful. Ricky went from managing a Burger King to selling cosmetics. As a "pretty boy" at the cosmetic counter interacting with the ladies was something he did best. In and out of a short marriage, and with three children spread among three women, Ricky didn't understand how a smart and personable guy like himself had gone nowhere fast. He had become a drug user, was divorced, was unemployed every other year, and didn't have a pot to piss in. Where did he go wrong?

Focus

Maybe it was in high school, when Ricky lost focus on his education and started thinking that college would be too hard. Some of the students from his high school went to college but most of them didn't. His grades were slipping and Ricky began thinking college might not be for him. Ricky wondered if not having any rules at home—for school work, bedtime or much of anything else—was part of his problem.

High school wasn't easy for J.R. either, but he had learned good study habits from his mother in sixth and seventh grade, and they had served him well. The benefits of keeping up with schoolwork, doing some homework every night and getting a good night's sleep helped him keep focus.

During high school, Ricky and J.R. still hung out on occasion, but it was clear that J.R. was a little more serious about school than Ricky. They both graduated from high school in the same year, and Ricky became a father a week after graduation. Both he and J.R. applied to two universities. J.R. applied to a big state school and a smaller college, while Ricky applied to only the big schools. College was in both of their futures, but at different schools, since J.R. got more scholarship money from the small school.

New Realities

J.R. wasn't too happy that he graduated from college in four and a half years, rather than in the traditional four, but he found out early that the system wasn't really set up for most students, especially black students, to graduate in four years. Graduating with a 3.1 grade point average had been hard work, but it definitely made it easier to go to law school.

Coming from high school with good grades wasn't enough to stop J.R.'s college counselor from recommending that he begin his freshman year in college with only 13 semester credit hours. She suggested that if J.R. did well enough in those classes, he might consider taking 16 semester hours in the second half of the school year. With 13 credit hours in the first semester and 16 in the second, J.R. would have 29 semester hours after his freshman year.

But there was one big problem with averaging 29 semester hours per year. In four years, J.R. would only have 116 semester hours, and he needed 126 hours to graduate. And the 116 hours was assuming that he never dropped a class in four years of college, which is highly unlikely. J.R. wondered if his white counterparts from the all-white high schools had received the same advice from the counselor. Or, had the university set up a program where everyone probably needed more than four years to graduate? It didn't really matter to him, but he sure found it odd that almost all of his black friends were starting their freshman year with only 13 hours.

J.R. had no interest in law until he took part in a mock trial in his senior year of high school. Getting into two law schools was a thrill for him. After graduating from law school with honors, J.R. interviewed with many law firms, and here he was, seven years later looking out over Lake Michigan as a partner with Robinson, Massey and Morris.

Nobody to Tell You What to Do

Ricky loved his only year of college. Like most college students, this was his first real time away from home. There was nobody to tell you what to do and Ricky loved that aspect of college best. There was no one to tell you to go to bed, no one to tell you to study, and not even anyone bothering you about going to class. And the parties were the best!

While under-aged drinking is illegal, it's probably most abused on college campuses, and Ricky took full advantage. At one party, he was so drunk, he didn't remember how he got back to his dorm room, or the name of the naked girl lying next to him when he finally woke up. Grades in college don't come easy and it's much harder when you only make it to class half the time. After first semester grades came out, Ricky began thinking that maybe college wasn't for him. Ricky began his freshman year with 13 semester hours, just like J.R. But after dropping a class, he finished with only 10 semester credits and had received very marginal grades.

Upon completing his freshman year, Ricky found himself on academic probation. He didn't catch the mail in time like he did after first semester, so his mom actually received his final grades before he did. She went ballistic! After all the things she had done for him, she was really pissed off. Whine, whine, nag, nag! That's all Ricky heard all summer long. And with just a little assistance from his mom, Ricky decided he wasn't going back to school. He could still hear her words clear as a bell, "If you're not going to do any better than this, then you might as well stay at home." And Ricky did.

The Choice Is Yours

So which son will you be raising? Is it J.R. or Ricky? Same could be said for Portia or Nina. As a parent or a parent-to-be, you can greatly improve the chances that your child will become a J.R. rather than a Ricky. You can make the difference. Which child will be yours? It's largely up to you.

Children today are more out of control than ever before. Parents have lost control of their children and seem to wonder why. Show me a child that's uncontrollable and, nine times out of ten, I'll show you a parent that has an opportunity to take more responsibility.

Parents often don't respect their children, and so it's not surprising that children don't respect their parents. These days, many parents let their children make parenting decisions. How ridiculous!

By investing a little time, energy and—on rare occasion—a little money, you can become a better parent. So if you're ready, let's go. It's time for you to get the perspective of *A Black Man Thinking, Volume One—Raising Children*.

2
It Begins with You

C onsider, that if you have a problem child, you are probably the answer to the problem. The old saying "the fruit
doesn't fall far from the tree" is particularly true with most
children. So if you have a problem child, it's probably because
of you.

"My daughter just doesn't seem to get it," Mark declared.

A long-time friend and I were having lunch when the subject of his daughter came up. We had discussed mutual friends,
business opportunities, some family stories and a host of other
things. When the discussion came around to his daughter,
Mark was passionate.

"I've tried to explain to her that her grades are very important and she'll need the good grades to get a good job so she
can keep the lifestyle that she has today. She comes home from

school and spends about an hour doing homework and then she turns on the television. Her older sister is there when she gets home from school and is supposed to help her, but sometimes I think she spends as much time in front of the TV as her younger sister. How much longer do I have to tell her that she has got to change in order to get better grades? Sometimes I don't think she's ever going to get it. What in the world should I do with her?"

This scenario probably applies to the parents of many high school and grammar school parents. If you're not yet a parent and are preparing for your first child, then you're way ahead of the game. The answer to the question lies within you. That's right, more often than not, the parent is the answer to what is wrong with the child.

My response to Mark was, "The answer is you."

"The answer is me?" he responded while he processed my statement.

"Yep, the answer is you," I repeated.

"Me?! But I already have my college diploma and my daughter hasn't gotten out of sixth grade," he said.

"Yeah Mark, you are largely responsible for changing the behavior in your child," I told him. "What have you done to put a support system in place for homework without the television? What rules have you put in place? And, what expectations have you set? In order to change the behavior in your child, you've got to change *your* behavior."

"That's deep," was Mark's reply. "I never thought of it like that."

Do as I Say ... and as I Do

There are many great old sayings that express pretty much the same thing:

- *More important than what you say is what you do.*
- *With children, it is much easier to understand that which is seen.*
- *More than 75 percent of all learning goes through the eyes, not the ears.*

So telling your child to do things that you don't do will not work. Telling your child not to watch television while you sit around and watch TV won't work. Telling your child to turn off the TV before they go to bed while you fall asleep regularly with the TV on, will not work. Telling your child not to smoke cigarettes while you're a regular smoker won't work. You'll be your child's role model, like it or not. So you must show your child the behavior that you'd most like to see in them.

No one can influence your child as much as you can, as long as you're spending quality time with your son or daughter. No one and nothing! It's very easy for children to get caught up in gangs and peer pressure if their parents aren't showing their children that they care and that they love them.

Your Opportunity to Shape a Life

As a parent, you have a great opportunity: the opportunity to shape a life. And if you take responsibility for your child, you can build a foundation that will withstand the test of time. Outside influences may negatively impact your bouncing bundle of joy. But it's your job to be involved in the lives of your children so those influences are not as important as yours.

None of this is nuclear physics, so it should be clear that *you* have to change if change is required with your child. More importantly, you'll have to see things just a little differently than you did before. You will have to change how you see, in your mind's eye, your child being raised. This vision should not be based on how you're living today or your current environment, but the environment you want for your child. You can do it, but the first step is that you have to want to do it.

> "Parents need to fill a child's bucket of self-esteem so high that the rest of the world can't poke enough holes in it to drain it dry."
>
> — ALVIN PRICE

My Vision

Your vision may be different from mine, but here are a few things I believe are important in coming up with a vision for children:

- Establish a code of values.
- Manage the TV, computers and other monitors.
- Schedule a regular family reading time.
- Make your home a smoke-free environment.
- Eat dinner together.
- Have fun as a family.
- Make spirituality a priority.

The list could go on and on, but I think you get the point. You are going to be responsible for how your child is raised and it all begins with you.

Lead the Way

You have to lead the way in setting a good example for your child, and behave the way you want your child to behave. Ex-NBA star Charles Barkley got it right when he said, "Professional athletes should not be role models." It's not that we don't want athletes to be good, outstanding citizens; it's just that they may not be, and they're not around your child enough to make a difference. Kobe Bryant may

> *"Our greatness lies not so much in being to remake the world ... as in being to remake ourselves."*
> — *Mohandas Gandhi*

be a good role model, but *only* on the basketball court. Parents should be the real role models.

Even as an infant, children can sense and pick up what's going on in the house. Who you are speaks much louder to your child than anything that comes out of your mouth. If you want to begin changing your situation, then you must change yourself, and to change effectively you must first see things differently.

One of my favorite books is Stephen Covey's *Seven Habits of Highly Effective People*. The aspect of changing yourself is addressed by Dr. Covey as the "inside-out" approach. In essence, you must first change your "inside" in order to make a true difference on the outside. In raising your child, changing your inside and how you think about things will be critical to your success.

Two-Parent Homes Are Best

> *"If you lie down with dogs, don't be surprised if you get up with fleas."*
>
> — UNKNOWN

Since this process begins with you, let's digress for a minute. Raising a child is hard work, and it's much harder for those raising children as a young, single parent. If you have a choice, and you typically do, try to raise your child in a two-parent home. These days, a two-parent home seems to be the exception, and you can be that exception.

The fact is that children raised in young, single-parent homes, usually without a father, have a much higher chance of not finishing high school, committing a crime, living in poverty and abusing drugs or alcohol. Girls who grow up without their fathers are more likely to become pregnant as teenagers.

Having a baby is the easiest part of the story. The more challenging task is to take responsibility for your choices, and to take responsibility for raising your child to the best of your ability. That other person involved in the baby-making exercise will always be your child's biological parent, and there is nothing you can do that will change that fact.

Keep Your Value High

When I was in college, my father shared a particularly good insight with me related to having sex. Once I started having sex (I was actually a sophomore in college), my behavior was just like a lot of guys when they started having sex. I wanted to have sex with as many girls as I could, and I was nineteen years old. My father recognized a change in my behavior, and told me something that has stayed with me ever since:

"You're worth a lot more if everyone doesn't know your stuff. Sleeping with a bunch of girls might seem like a lot of fun, but your value will keep going down. The more girls you have sex with, the lower your value. And if you sleep with only one girl, you'll find that your value will go up. To find the type of women I know you'd like, I can guarantee you that you want your value to be as high as possible."

After that conversation, I became much more particular about having sex, and remember, I was nineteen years old. Today, many children have sex at a much earlier age. At fifteen or sixteen, you're not as smart as you'll be at nineteen, and the choices will be harder to make. And I'm not suggesting the choices are easy at nineteen, but they're a lot easier to make then at sixteen.

The point is that you should choose your sex partners wisely. Based on your previous choices, you may have to make a decision as to if you'll be raising your child in a single-parent home. No doubt about it, a good two-parent home will always be better for your child than a good single-parent home. But a bad two-parent home isn't any good at all. Regardless of your choice, get comfortable with the decisions you've made and make a plan for the best means of moving forward.

Making the Best of Single-Parenthood

If your child is raised in a single-parent home, understand that you cannot take the place of the other parent. The best father cannot take the place of a mother, and since so many black children are raised by young single mothers, let me make it clear that a mother cannot take the place of a father. Just as much as girls need their mothers, boys need their fathers, too. Even the best single mom on the planet can never take a father's place with their son.

According to the *Statistical Abstract of the United States: 2006*, almost 45 percent of black families had a female head of household with no spouse present, versus 15 percent for whites.

While the percentage of black children raised in homes below the poverty level has decreased to 34 percent from a high in the mid-40s in 1992, the black percentage is still more than double the percentage of white children. You probably won't be surprised to find that while there are many issues associated with poverty, there is a direct relationship between poverty and being raised in a single-parent home.

These statistics don't mean that a child raised in a single-parent home won't become a success, but it does mean that the odds against success are greater. One of the biggest issues facing black children is the lack of two-parent families.

In my opinion, it's not OK to plan on being a young, single parent. If the hand you're dealt means you'll be a single mom or dad, then be the best single parent that you can be. But let's not outwardly suggest that being a young, single parent is behavior we expect. We should strive to encourage two-parent households in the black community; instead, it feels as if we've set up a huge system to help support young, single parents. While I'm not against supporting young, single parents, I'm against advocating that young boys and girls should think it's alright to have children without a plan to get married, or that young, black girls should plan on raising their children alone.

Setting the Wrong Standard

Pregnant high school girls often have elaborate baby showers, sometimes given by one of their parents. And everybody says how nice it is that they're having a baby. What? This is the type of support system that drives the wrong behavior. Younger girls observing a big baby shower with all the gifts and the congratulations could easily think that having a baby in high school is pretty cool. Do big baby showers for high school mothers enable the behavior we should be discouraging? I think they do.

One of the objectives of every young girl should be that she will not get pregnant before getting a high school diploma. No young girls should go around thinking its OK to get pregnant while in high school. There shouldn't be groups of young girls in high schools across America deciding that they'll have babies while still in high school. And sadly, girls across America are doing just that.

But let's not absolve young men from responsibility in this single-parent syndrome. Young men have a responsibility to raise their children as best they can. While young men only have veto power *before* the baby making exercise, they can still carry much influence over the situation and the outcome. Is the one you're with someone with whom you'd like to marry and raise a child? Is this female someone you'd want to have your baby with, planned or otherwise?

The Reality of Teen Parenthood

Being a high school parent is very hard work, and typically high school fathers quickly fall out of the family picture with basketball, friends, schoolwork and just hanging out. And then the burden falls squarely on the young, single, high school mom and her parents or support system.

As a high school parent, your child is most likely to be raised in a single-parent household, which makes everything a lot harder. You'll need a good support system, since you'll have to finish high school and hopefully go on to college. But the tricky part of being a teen parent is when it's time to start hanging out again. At seventeen, you'll most likely start leaving your child with either a sitter or a grandmother so that you can hang out with your friends. The transition from hanging out every now and then to leaving your child with his or her grandparent on a regular basis is very easy. And when you look back, you'll see that you have put your child in the space of many black children: being raised by grandparents.

It's not easy being a grandparent and raising your child's child. Grandparents were put on the earth to love their grandchildren unconditionally, spoil them as best they can, and then send them back to their parents. A grandparent's job is not to instill discipline in their grandchildren, even though many will do so successfully. The best thing that happens to many children is grandparents, so I'm not knocking grandparents. It's just not their job to raise your children, it's yours.

Take Responsibility for Your Choices

Nonetheless, stuff happens, and if you find yourself raising a child in a single-parent home, understand that the choices you made will be taking over your life. Take responsibility and understand that your work will be harder as a single parent. Good things can still happen, but only if you take responsibility, both for your previous choices and for raising your child to the best of your ability.

> *"You must be the change you wish to see in the world."*
> — MOHANDAS GANDHI

Many very successful people were raised in single-parent homes, so your child's success is not solely based on the number of parents in the household. It only becomes more critical that you put the proper foundation in place for your child to succeed. Many successful business people and celebrities were raised in single-parent homes. So the success of a child will not be based solely on being raised in one type of household over another. It is much more important to establish values and have high standards for your children. That's where a role model can be very beneficial.

Role Model Behavior

Having a role model for a child is always a very good thing. Hopefully you can be your child's role model, but if you're a single mom it will be difficult for you to be a role model if you have a son. While single women can effectively raise boys, it's important for boys to have a male role model. Role models for your son can come in many forms and certainly don't have to be their father, even though that's preferred. A male role model is critical for boys, so seek the best one you can if you're a single mom. You might find that role model at your place of worship, an after school program or involved in a Parent Teacher Organization. If you get involved in organizations whose objective is to help others, you'll often discover potential role models. That role model could be for your child or a parental role model for you.

Try to find either a parent like the parent you want to be, or find a child that is like the child you want yours to become. Once you find that behavior, try to copy it. Meet with the parent and tell them that you like how they've raised their child and you'd like to know how they did it. You'll get all kinds of great suggestions and possibly a mentor, but more importantly another parent whose advice you can use.

When my wife and I moved into our home a few months after getting married, we found our role models. Our next door neighbors, Gary and Betty Wiley had two of the most articulate and personable young children I had ever met. After a month or two of observing Jenny and Kevin Wiley, my wife told me "Mo, that's how I want *our* children to be!" We didn't have children at the time, but we had found our role model children.

You can find role models too! Having role models can help you in seeing a different future for your children and dreaming of what could be.

Have a Vision for Your Child

Dream of what your child can become if you set the proper foundation. Becoming the chief executive officer (CEO) of a Fortune 500 company can be within the reach of your child. Your child could become an entrepreneur who employs thousands of people while serving the community. Serving God may be your child's gift. Becoming a doctor, a lawyer or an astronaut, could also be within your child's reach. Your child can become successful in any of these roles if you set the proper foundation. The proper foundation should support your vision.

Now take another look at your vision. If you're sure that your vision will be best for you and your child, then write it down and stick to it. Make sure it passes a sanity check, and if it does, then lock it in. *Everything you do and everything you are should support your vision.*

Make Changes in Your Own Life First

Now that you've given some thought to your vision, you'll have to determine the changes you'll have to make to reach your goal of achieving that vision. For our purposes, your goal is to have the lifestyle and environment that will be best to raise a healthy and happy child. In planning, you will have to determine what you'll have to change to attain your goal.

Begin with leading a life that is an example for your child. Children must learn values from you. Your lifestyle must be centered with values that are important to you. Share your values by the way you live. Honesty, reliability, respect, accountability and responsibility are just a few of the fundamental values.

Take good care of yourself from a physical and mental perspective. Relaxation is a lost art, and that doesn't mean sitting in front of the dreaded television. Exercise something other than your options. Eat healthy foods to set a good example. Be involved in your community and in your place of worship. Your spirit needs nourishment as well, so please feed it accordingly.

As your child grows, make sure you have defined what success looks like for both you and your child. Put your house in order and live your life like you'd like your child to live his or hers.

> *"The golden opportunity you are seeking is in yourself"*
> — MARY ENGELBREIT

Instill Pride in Your Child

Your job as a parent is to instill the critical values in your bundle of joy. This includes teaching them social skills as simple as getting along with others and having pride in all they do. As a black parent, pride is critical for our children, and like it or not, race matters.

Teach your children about black history. Many children today don't have a clue about the civil rights struggles and the battles fought by their grandparents. Tell your children any valuable stories that you know about the struggles of black people in America and the power of voting. If you don't know about these stories, then go to a library and read a few articles or books on black history. When people don't understand the past, they tend to take things for granted. Set the stage so your child understands the importance of education and the many struggles of black people in a time not so long ago.

"Black Is My Favorite Color"

Learning colors is one of those things that your child will probably learn at a fairly early age. My son came home one day from school and asked me, "What is your favorite color?"

After a short pause, I responded, "Black is my favorite color. I love black and all my favorite clothes are black."

The next day, my son came home a little disappointed and informed me, "My teacher said black is not a color, and black is the absence of color, so what is your favorite color?"

"Tell your teacher that black is your father's favorite color," I said. "My favorite shoes are black, my favorite coat is black, our car is black and my favorite pants are black. So please tell your teacher that black *is* your father's favorite color."

As a black child, I didn't want my son to think of black as the absence of color. Black is very much a color in the world of black Americans, and I thought it was important that my son got comfortable with black as a color. You must teach your child those lessons that are important to you. Tell your children your story, it's a great way to connect with a child.

You've also got to decide what you feel is important for your child to learn from you. If your child obtains respect, responsibility, hard work, accountability, honesty and reliability in their early years, it will be largely because of you.

Get Started and Stay Focused

The biggest barrier to your success in changing your habits and lifestyle will be your ability to get started and to stay focused. There will be naysayers and others providing hurdles to stop you from achieving your goal of changing your lifestyle in a way that supports your vision for your child, and that's OK.

You should plan on being your child's biggest fan. Never say a discouraging word about your child. Every area of concern or trouble should be thought of as an opportunity for both you and your child to get better or smarter. You may even encounter people who try to take advantage of your child. Never, ever let anyone take advantage of your child.

> *"There is no such thing in anyone's life as an unimportant day".*
> — *ALEXANDER WOOLLCOTT*

You'll also find that there are those that will try to get you off your path, or say that trying to change something is crazy. Don't listen to them for a minute. Even if you've shared your dreams with friends, you're the one who must work toward those dreams. Your vision is your vision, and only you know all of your experiences in life. Lock in on your vision and don't let go! Your vision is where you want to end up, and all roads won't get you there. Some of your friends may even be your biggest roadblock.

Your so-called friends and acquaintances can't stop you if you're determined to make the changes that you see fit. Remember that any changes you have chosen to make are all about you and your child, and you are responsible. The easiest thing about working on you is that you are in control of your biggest obstacle, because when all is said and done, the biggest obstacle is probably you.

Today is the day for you to get started working your plan, and taking action to implement the changes you have determined. It all depends on you, and you can do it! We're only talking about being the best parent you can be. And although it takes very little money, it does take time. Step up to the challenge, you can do it. Get started today.

Take This with You:

- *Have a vision and write it down.*
- *Be consistent and stay determined.*
- *You are the answer.*

And Remember:

- *Write down your goals.*
- *Make a plan.*
- *Take action.*

3
The Environment

You don't have to live like the Huxtables on *The (Bill) Cosby Show* to provide a good environment for your child. But keep in mind that what you do and how you do it will greatly influence your children.

So, if you're a smoker, there's a good chance your child will smoke. If you're a reader, there's a good chance your child will be a reader. If you're an optimist, it's a good chance your child will be an optimist. Most children become products of their environment, and you have the chance to create that environment.

en-vi-ron-ment   *1: the surrounding conditions or forces that influence or modify*
2: the social and cultural conditions that influence the life of a person

Take Control, Manage Your Child's Environment

Raising your children will be so much easier if you manage their environment. Take control of the conditions, where you can, that will influence your son or daughter. Since there are so many things that can influence a child today, it's important to remember that you are the parent, and you probably know better than your young child what's best. It seems that many parents often forget that they are the parents. It's great to be a friend to your children, but your primary role must be that of a parent. So cherish your role and use common sense.

Some parents seem to negotiate almost everything with their children. Don't negotiate if a jacket is needed when you've already checked the weather forecast and you know it's going to rain. If you haven't checked the forecast, then you should do so before your child walks out the door. There is no need to negotiate.

Often parents let children make parenting decisions, and that's just wrong. Children shouldn't decide if their friends should come to visit. Children shouldn't determine if they need to do their homework or wash the dishes. Children shouldn't determine if they should go to church or to a place of worship. These are all parenting decisions, so don't negotiate when you know what's best. *You* are the parent. *You* get to decide.

In today's world, children are influenced by their friends, television, music, movies and their surroundings at home, all of which make up their environment. Make a point to control what you can, influence what you can, and let the rest go.

The major environmental factors are parents and extended family, friends, books, music and things that need a monitor. Television is typically watched via a monitor. Video games, cell phones, iPods and the Internet all use monitors. You've got to take responsibility to manage these factors and set appropriate limits.

The family and friends that your children observe every day will have an impact on their lives. Don't let family and friends show your children behaviors in which you don't approve. Hearing friends of yours curse at each other or talk in mean tones will send a bad example to your child long before they can walk or talk. The bad language that's commonplace in many communities is poisoning our youth. That's one of the reasons why children think it's acceptable to speak poorly, or in disrespectful tones, or use curse words. Be aware of the things your child is hearing.

You can manage the friends, and to a lesser extent, the family, that come in contact with your child, and you should. It is important for you to understand that your child is like a sponge and will soak up everything around them. Soak up the environment, the values, the language, the fun and the love. What happens in your home will become your child's foundation. What you do in your home will come out in your child.

Shower Your Child with Love, Not Money

Love is a verb. Show everyone in your house that you love them. All children can feel the love or the lack of love in a home. Children will also go someplace else looking for love if they're not getting it at home, and they'll find it somewhere. Be it a classmate, a gang, an Internet buddy, or a neighbor, your child will seek love and find it elsewhere if you're not providing the love they need at home.

Show your love. Shower your child with kisses and hugs everyday. Always tell your child that you love them, and back that up with patience and sensitivity. You should be your child's biggest cheerleader and help to build their confidence. Smile. Listen to your child and don't assume that you know all the answers. And once again, spend time with your child. Communicating with your child becomes much easier when you spend quality time together going to museums, to the park, or simply talking over dinner.

Showing love doesn't necessarily mean spending money. Plan on spending time with your children doing activities that both of you enjoy. If you can't find something both of you like, then do something your child will like. But it's still your choice. It's a very small sacrifice for you and will be well worth the effort. Life is often about making small sacrifices, and you'll have many opportunities to sacrifice for your child. You could take a trip to the park to play catch, kick a ball, or swing on the swings. A trip to the museum might be interesting and fun. The most important thing you can spend with your child is time, not money. There will be times when you will have to open your pocket for some cash to go to a movie or something, but spending money should be the exception, not the rule. Your child probably doesn't need a pair of hundred dollar athletic shoes as much as he or she needs your time.

val-ue   1: *the worth, desirability, or utility of a thing*
             2: *one's principles or standards; one's judgment of what is valuable or important in life*

Set a Good Example

Try to live your life based on the values you want your child to have. Honesty, responsibility and trust are just a few of the core values that are most important to your child's foundation. Your child will see if you are not responsible or honest. It is very hard to raise a responsible and honest child unless you raise your child in a responsible and honest environment. These core values are your responsibility.

Buying stolen items off a truck or from the guy on the corner to save a few dollars will show your children bad behavior. Purchasing bootlegged movies from the barbershop is supporting illegal, bad behavior and your children are watching.

Talk to your children about these values and all the others that are important to you. These values will become a part of your "House Rules," so choose them wisely. Values should be communicated both in what you do and in what you say. Take the time, preferably at an early age, to explain why each value is important to you and why these values are important for your children. Each time you find your children living these values, let them know you're proud of them and why. Never miss a chance to recognize when your children do something right, and tell them in a positive and loving way.

Turn Off the "Boob Tube"

Television is probably the biggest outside influence in many children's lives. The biggest problem with TV and other forms of media is that they take time away from other activities that sharpen the mind, like reading. I'm going to focus on television and its influences because it is poisoning our youth.

While TV can be a very useful tool, there is a good reason it is sometimes known as the "boob tube." You sit and watch television, and when you're done, you get up and walk away and rarely are you better or smarter than when you first sat down. Most people use the TV as a means of entertainment and don't take into account the values, the clothes, and the lifestyles that the TV brings into their home. And that's why we have a generation of children with values based on what they've seen or heard on TV or from others, rather than from their parents.

It's up to you to take responsibility for your child's values and not leave it up to the television. Never let television determine how your children speak to adults—*you* should make that determination. Respect is a value that is clearly lacking in many television shows, and you have to have respect in your household.

Respect Starts at Home

One of the responsibilities of being a parent is that you get to set the rules. So you get to decide the house rules and things like how your children should address you. Don't let your child decide what they want to call you. You decide.

I'm not a proponent for children calling their parents by their first names. If your child is calling you by your first name, you'll soon find that they'll use tones just like when they're talking to their friends. And sometimes those tones will be downright disrespectful, and you've got to have respect. Running a household is not a democracy, and it should have a clear hierarchy. You don't address the king or queen as Charles or Elizabeth, and children shouldn't address their parents on a first name basis either. That first name stuff makes it seem as if you and your child might be peers, and while you might like to be your child's best friend, it's more important that you be their parent first.

> *"Either you manage the environment or the environment manages you."*
> — MAURICE ARTHUR

You shouldn't let television dictate what your child wears. Don't let television motivate your children to feel they need tattoos or body piercing. The same goes for music. Don't let 50 Cent make it seem like it's alright to wear pants hanging down to your knees with underwear showing. It's not alright, and you shouldn't allow such behavior in your house.

Too Much TV Poses New Threat for Youth

Managing television viewing in your home is a great place to start. According to one study, a third of black twelfth-graders spend five or more hours watching TV on school nights. That's five times more than whites, and twice as much as Latinos.

Most households in the United States do not have rules related to television viewing, and this can greatly damage children.

Our world has changed a lot in the last twenty years. Back then, there were only a few television stations to choose from, so often there really wasn't anything "good" to watch. It didn't take much for a parent to monitor the TV watching, since there were usually only one or two televisions in the house, and it was rare to have a television in a child's bedroom. There was actually a time when the television stations stopped showing programs. You knew you had stayed up late when you saw the American flag on the screen with the Star-Spangled Banner playing before the screen went to static. Yes, there was actually a time when television went off!

Today with satellite and cable TV, there are hundreds of stations from which to choose. With so many choices, you can almost always find something to watch. Not to mention that television programming is now available twenty-four hours a day, seven days a week and 365 days a year. With so much to choose from and twenty-four/seven availability, a parent's job is much more difficult than before. The cost of a television is no longer an issue, so it's not uncommon to have three or more televisions in a house. With all those televisions in the house, many times televisions find their way into children's bedrooms, where it's virtually impossible to monitor viewing habits.

So keep those televisions out of your child's bedroom. Once the television is in a child's bedroom, you have lost a good deal of control. You won't know what shows your child is watching or when. While on the subject of a child's bedroom, keep Internet access out of the bedroom as well. The Internet is a powerful tool, but unrestricted access to the Internet is not good for children. When I speak of managing the monitors, the television and the Internet are at the top of the list, and I strongly suggest you keep both out of your child's bedroom.

In the 1960s and 1970s, your television choices ranged from *The Dick Van Dyke Show* to *Bonanza*, with relatively wholesome movies on *Family Classics*. If you liked a little more excitement, you may have watched the *Twilight Zone* or the *Outer Limits*. There was no MTV, VH1 or BET. There were no "shake yo booty" videos, and no visual pictures of young black men dressed liked thugs with do-rags on their heads and their jeans hanging low. While it has never been easy raising a black child in America, back then it was a lot easier because you didn't have so many outside influences impacting your child.

Today, the choices are extreme and potentially damaging. With the advent of reality TV shows, your child can watch something senseless virtually every hour of every day. The current television environment makes it much easier for your child to pick up values that are not yours and act in ways that you won't like. The current television environment also means that if you don't monitor television viewing in your home, then the TV will rule your house. The values of *The Jerry Springer Show* in the U.S. or *The Jeremy Kyle Show* in the U.K. need not be the values in your home. And remember, it's your choice.

Sell, Sell, Sell

Letting the television and the commercials dictate your child's expectations may get you and your child into a lot of trouble. Television programming is one thing, since the attempt is to entertain you, but television commercials are another. Commercials are made solely for the purpose of attempting to sell something. Commercials are made to influence a buying decision and to change the way you think about a product or service. They are trying to sell you something. Millions of advertising research dollars have been spent to determine what sells, and the answer probably won't surprise you. Sex sells!

Studies have linked excessive TV viewing to obesity, early sexual activity and increased violence. Many of the commercials are targeted to males eighteen to thirty-five years old, so you should understand why you'll see so many sexual innuendos. Your son or daughter will be picking up the sexual vibe too, so it's no wonder that excessive TV watching will get children interested in sex at an earlier age.

A recent Kaiser Foundation report found that 70 percent of all TV programming contained sexual content, and that the number of scenes involving sex has doubled in the last five years. The same study also found that only 14 percent of TV shows with sexual content refer to sexual risks or responsibilities.

The message these shows send to children is that it's appropriate to be sexually active with little risk and no responsibility. These are not the messages that you want your child to receive, and *you* have to make them aware of the risks and the responsibilities that come with sex. Remember, *you* have to be the one that most influences your child, not TV, commercials, the Internet or their friends.

Children are easy to influence and TV commercials are built to influence. The average child sees 40,000 commercials a year. That's 40,000 messages that are trying to change how one thinks, how your child will think. Since the average black child watches more TV than average, you can bump the commercials up to 45,000 or 50,000. That's mind-boggling! So let's see some of the messages that will be bombarding your child.

In an hour of television viewing, you could easily see commercials selling fast food, expensive athletic shoes, cell phones, Internet services, cars and drugs to do just about anything. Drugs to help you lose weight, control menstrual pains, get rid of your headache or to resolve erectile dysfunction.

"Mommy, what's erectile dysfunction?"

That is not a question you want your six-year-old daughter asking you, but with the commercials of today, the question can easily come up. Some of the manufacturers of these drugs even sponsor sporting events, with commercials touting their products at 2 pm on Sunday afternoons. And as my buddy Duane stated, "Just wait, someone will soon name their daughter Levitra."

Commercials are made to influence, so it's not surprising to end up with an overweight child who loves fast food, drinks beer, and wants $100 sneakers, a car, and must have a cell phone—all before his or her sixteenth birthday. Advertisers will spend billions of dollars targeting their advertising at your children and teens.

You can't stop these messages from getting through to your child, but you can limit the messages, and you can lay a strong foundation in your child so that commercials won't determine your child's values.

A Lesson from Mrs. Bashyal

Once upon a time, I went to see my son's teacher, Mrs. Bashyal, for a preschool parent-teacher conference. I was pretty happy with how my wife and I were raising our son, and I asked his teacher if there was anything we could do better in working with my son. Be careful when you ask this type of question, because you may not like the answer. After thinking about it for a minute, Mrs. Bashyal suggested that we turn off the television in the morning before bringing my son to school. I was a bit surprised at her comments and wondered how she knew my son watched television in the morning. Like many parents, my wife and I often sat my son in front of the television for fifteen to thirty minutes in the morning while we were getting ready for work.

Mrs. Bashyal told me that she could tell which children had watched television before school and which children had not, based solely on their behavior.

"Really?" was my response.

"Sure," she said.

Then I jumped to the more important question that popped into my mind, "Was my son acting up in class?"

"Oh no ..." was her reply, "but the children who watch television in the morning are much more active when they get to school and not in the right frame of mind to learn."

I was shocked. No, I guess I was really stunned. Sure, she had been teaching children for twenty to twenty-five years, but I was still surprised by her statement about the television, and right then and there, I decided that the television would be off in the morning. If that meant we had to get up a little earlier to deal with my son while we got dressed in the morning, then so be it. And that was the beginning of managing the television in my home.

While my son's early morning television watching meant he was a little too active when he got to school, I quickly realized the impact that the television could have in the household. If watching *Sesame Street* in the morning could alter behavior, it was easy for me to see the damage that constant television watching could have on both children and adults. I wonder what would have happened if my child were watching something with a little more sex and violence than *Sesame Street* in the morning.

That preschool television experience changed the TV-watching in my home for good. We quickly modified our television watching so that we didn't watch TV on Monday through Thursday. My children didn't have a problem with the "no TV during the week" policy, since that was how they were raised. Of course, we let the children watch some TV if there was a particular show that they wanted to watch, but typically the TV was off during the week.

According to a Kaiser study, 68 percent of U.S. children two and under spend an average of two hours a day watching TV, videos or DVDs. Furthermore, children who spend more time watching TV have more trouble learning how to read.

A Call from Home

A couple of years ago, I was with a few people from my job when my cell phone rang.

"Dad, I've finished my homework and there is a program on TV this evening called *The West Wing* that I heard was good, so is it alright for me to watch it?"

My son was fifteen or sixteen at the time, and while I hadn't seen the show, I had heard it was very good.

"Sure," was my reply.

After ending the conversation, I turned to one of my co-workers and mentioned the show and that my son wanted to watch some TV this evening.

"How do you know that your children don't watch TV when you're not home?" was a question from one of my co-workers.

"My children won't watch TV if they know they're not supposed to," was my reply.

"There's no way I could trust my kids to not watch TV if I weren't home," said my co-worker.

"That's because your children weren't raised that way," I stated.

To this day, my children will still call me to see if it's OK to turn on the TV during the school week, and they're eighteen and fourteen years old.

Manage "Monitor Time" at Home

You can determine some of your child's habits—and television watching is nothing more than a habit. Television watching is a bad habit, if you ask me, but a habit nonetheless. Children watch too much television, and it is up to you to help them break the habit.

We've already established that recent studies have shown that black children watch more TV than whites or Hispanics. Studies have also linked excessive TV viewing to obesity, poor body image, attention disorders, substance abuse, early sexual activity and increased violence, according to the American Academy of Pediatrics. What other evidence do you need?

I'm a believer that children should not have televisions in their bedroom. A recent survey revealed that two-thirds of all teenage children had televisions in their bedrooms and averaged six and a half hours of TV-watching a day, seven days a week in front of a monitor. It's no wonder that so many children get most of their values from one monitor or another.

"You may be disappointed if you fail, but you are doomed if you don't try."
— BEVERLY SILLS

So try this at home, begin managing the television watching in your home. Have a day or two per week when you don't turn on the television. There might be some initial shock from family members, but you'll find that turning off the television will open up other avenues for discussion and **more time for reading**. Start slowly and get buy-in from the children. Find out what days they would like to watch a TV program, and then determine what days you'll designate as no-TV days. You'll be surprised at the results.

You may have to modify your rules as your children get older. While TV time was managed in my house, I had to expand the rules from television time to monitor time. With all the time that's spent watching DVDs, surfing the Internet, or playing X-Box or Playstation, I found it necessary to manage monitor time.

So the time limits initially placed on television viewing were expanded to include video games, the Internet and any other experience that requires a monitor.

Some Video Games Celebrate No Values, No Responsibility

Since video games are now a multi-billion dollar business, you should understand some of the dynamics of the video game industry.

Halo 2 made $125 million on the first day it hit the market, making it the biggest selling video game or movie of all time. *Grand Theft Auto-San Andreas* made more money in its opening weekend than the Harry Potter movie that opened in the same time frame. Best-selling video games have outsold the biggest of movies.

$10.5 billion dollars was generated in video game sales in 2005. For those of you like me, who like to see the numbers, that's $10,500,000,000. That's a lot of zeros! Now you can tell that video game sales are big, big business. It's the video game business that you'll also be fighting for the values of your child. It's not much of a fight at all, if you do your job as a parent in putting those values in your child at an early age. If your child has a set of core values, those video games will mean nothing to them. But if you haven't instilled those values, video games can alter how your child sees life and what they value. You don't want a $10 billion business determining your child's values. That wouldn't be a smart thing to do.

Take *Grand Theft Auto-San Andreas*, for instance.

It appears that the key objectives of this game are to: a) make as much money as you can, b) gain power and, c) kill people who get in your way, or who happen to piss you off.

In the game, you make money by committing a crime. Destroying public property, carjacking, robbing banks, and starting a gang war are all at your disposal. Once you have some money, you can buy guns to kill people as they get in your way, or just because.

You can hijack a car to sell. Then, you take the money and buy some guns to rob a bank. You might have to kill a few people leaving the bank and even a policeman if he tries to stop you. If two policemen are killed, an entire police squad would be after you instead of the one patrol car. The money from the bank robbery is used to buy a film studio. Not just any studio, but a porn film studio. But the porn film studio turns out to be a problem because it isn't making money. You know you aren't making money because the counter on the outside of the building tells you how much money you're making or losing. You end up having to kill a pimp because you need one of his prostitutes to make a good porn film so the studio can make money, or is it a strip club?

Nonetheless, using the new girl from the pimp you killed, you start making money. Earlier, you had visited a strip club and found that you couldn't start making money until you paid the stripper $500. After paying the $500, the money starts rolling in, so you learn the lesson that sometimes it takes money to make money. There's sex everywhere and the video images of the stripper dancing is almost lifelike. Life is good. You start a gang war, do a couple of drive-by shootings, and pick up some other guys who also have done drive-by shootings. You kill a couple of other cops and finally get killed by a SWAT unit as you try to hijack a plane. Getting killed is a drag, but no worries. Hit the restart button and you're on your way again.

In the world of some video games, there are no values, and there is no responsibility. Being a criminal is cool, and you can kill someone for any reason or no reason at all. There is no reason to respect authority or even to respect yourself. Laws are meant to be broken, and life has no meaning. Women can be mistreated and are portrayed as sex objects. Life has little value, or no value, other than the money you've acquired.

If your child is getting his or her values from these types of video games, and many children do, then you're going to have one screwed-up child with little or no respect for themselves or anyone else. Video games won't change your child's values if they already have good values instilled in them, but if they don't already have these values, you need to understand what you'll be dealing with. Children are spending too much time playing video games. It is up to you to limit video game access for your child, and start instilling your own values.

One thing video games don't provide is much in the way of dialogue or conversation. Pimps, whores and bitches aren't words you'll typically hear in the video games. But your child can get that and much more from music lyrics.

Another Threat to Values

Much of popular black music lyrics, and specifically I mean rap and hip-hop, is appalling. Not all of the lyrics, but a great deal of them. The lyrics are full of sex and violence and you probably don't want your fourteen-year-old son or daughter looking for a life of sex and violence. There is some good music and R&B is making a small comeback, but the lyrics of rap and hip-hop are still pervasive.

Much of today's music lyrics are explicit with sex, drugs, alcohol and more sex. There is nothing left to the imagination, and children are now being exposed to language that they shouldn't hear until they're adults, if even then.

Music can be soothing, and music can be fun. Music can be spiritual, or music can be violent. Your best defense against the forces of the music that will be bombarding your house is to instill sound family values in your children, and then the music won't matter. But there's nothing like feeling good when listening to music.

> *"Be a yardstick of quality. Some people aren't used to an environment where excellence is expected."*
>
> — STEVE JOBS

I'm definitely old-school and we still play lots of music in my house. Motown and traditional R&B are prevalent, with a smattering of the latest stuff. There is nothing more fun than to hear my family in a chorus of *I Heard It through the Grapevine* or *My Girl*. We never asked the children to sing along or learn the words to a song. It's the behavior they had observed, and they found it to be fun. That doesn't mean 50 Cent, Ja Rule, Jay-Z or any of the rest aren't played in the house. My children know most of the popular hip-hop songs, and I actually like a few. If you lay the proper foundation with your child, the music won't influence them very much.

Manage the Environment on All Fronts

Your children will become a product of their environment, so you've got to manage it. Influence the type of children that your child hangs out with. Determine their after-school activities and keep them involved in activities such as organized sports and church functions.

Children who hang out with A-students in school often become an A-student themselves. And students that associate with C-students typically become C-students. Stay in touch with your child's friends and school activities. Get involved in your child's school. Stay involved in your child's education.

It's a fact that black parents, as a whole, are more trusting of schools than white parents. Black households are much more likely than whites to think that education is the job for teachers. Your child's education is your job, first and foremost. You haven't done your job if you think you've done your share just by sending Junior to school. Attend parent-teacher conferences. An interesting thing about teachers is that they will work harder with your child if they know *you're* also working with your child. Attending parent-teacher conferences is a means of letting the teacher know that you care.

Set up a time and place for your children to do homework and **check their homework**. If your child sees that you care about their education and that you care enough to be involved, your child will try to please you and will work harder for you. The fact is that going to school is important for their future, and initially they'll want to get those good grades to please you. Not until late in high school will they figure out that the good grades are not only for you, but good for them as well.

There are so many aspects of the environment that, as a parent, you can control. You can really make a big difference in your child's life if you exercise that control. Please do.

Your role is vital in managing the environment in which your child lives and the media to which they're exposed. You may be the difference between your child being a success, or just being. Manage your environment and the monitors in your home, while instilling the important values in your child so Maury Povich, Trisha Goddard or Nelly doesn't have to.

Most of it is up to you. **You can do it!**

Take This with You:

- *Control your surroundings.*
- *Manage the monitors in your home.*
- *Influence your child more than anyone else.*

And Remember:

- *Set daily limits for TV, video games and the Internet.*
- *Provide balance by supporting activities such as reading, puzzles and board games.*
- *Be consistent and communicate.*

4
House Rules

Anyone who comes into your house must abide by the rules you've established in your home. Establishing house rules will set the framework for good behavior. These rules are not only for your children, but for anyone who comes into your home. The house rules are also a means for you to establish daily expectations. Managing the expectations of acceptability in your own home via house rules will set the structure that *you* have determined.

rule   *1: an authoritative direction for conduct or procedure*
         2: an established standard or habit of behavior

It's important to establish your own house rules, because you'll find every house and every child has slightly different guidelines, and sometimes no rules at all. When a person enters your house, they *must* abide by your rules. Note that I stated when a "person enters your house," not just a child. House rules apply for both visiting adults and children.

My children know that they need to "let their friends know" that boys don't wear baseball caps in our house. If any male, that's right, *any* male comes into the house wearing *any* headgear (boys wearing head scarves are included), they need to rest their cap or their scarf at the door. That's simply because it's a house rule, and we don't wear caps in the house. You can make that a house rule very easily, and in no time at all, you'll find that you're comfortable asking young men and their fathers to rest their caps. It also sets the expectation to be respectful in your house and in your presence. It really works. Try it!

Some House Rules

House rules also include values such as respect and honesty, as well as other guidelines you've established for your home. A few of my other house rules include the following:

- No bad language or cursing
- No underwear showing
- No running
- Must say a blessing before eating
- No negative or harsh tones when speaking
- No drugs
- Honesty
- No under-age drinking
- All children have a curfew

These are just a few of our house rules, and if you ask my children, they're likely to add quite a few others. The ones noted above are the clearly defined rules, but based on these rules, there are many de facto rules that sometimes come into play. A de facto rule is one that has become a rule through commonsense and circumstance. For instance, when children come into the house, they must speak to any adults in the house. And before they leave, they have to say goodbye. This wasn't always a rule in our house, but it became one through commonsense.

In raising children, you'll find all sorts of variations, so you'll have to be flexible in those circumstances that don't fit the established rules. Be flexible, but not stupid; the objective is to have well-defined boundaries where it will be clear that both you and your child will know when they have stepped over the line.

You might think that with all these rules, children wouldn't want to visit our house, but you'd be wrong. Children loved coming over because they quickly found that they could have lots of fun, as long as they were within our house rules.

An interesting fact is that the main enforcers for our house rules were my children. Once they understood how much fun they could have within the rules, they adapted and made sure other children stayed within our rules. Soon, my nephews and nieces understood the rules and always loved to visit.

In those instances when children came over that weren't familiar with our rules, either my children, or my nieces and nephews quickly made them aware. No one wanted their fun to end because some out-of-control child was misbehaving.

They were having too much fun! You see, you can have a house with rules and still have a home where children like to hang-out. That's the type of home you want yours to be.

Get Involved, Stay Involved

"You need to be in bed by 10 pm," my wife told our teen-age son one evening. "You're taking a big test tomorrow."

"Mom, that's earlier than my normal bedtime," was his response.

"That's OK, be in bed by 10 pm," she said.

End of discussion.

So you have to be involved in your son's education to know he has a big test the next day, and to set an appropriate time for bed. Most teenagers don't know a good time for bed, so you must set appropriate guidelines for them. Knowing they have school the next day and making sure they eat something before going to school for the big test is your job. All of these elements are within your control. Your son or daughter will do better on that test just because of the support structure *you* put around it. And a part of setting up that support is setting a bed time for a teenager.

If my son wasn't in bed by 10 pm, he had stepped over the line. Period. Time boundaries make it clear when a line has been crossed.

Regardless of the age of your children, set boundaries and set rules. Boundaries set the framework and rules determine what can happen within that framework. For instance, in basketball, the lines that determine the area of the court are boundaries. The rules of basketball determine what can happen within the boundaries:

- Five players on the court per team.
- One basketball.
- Rims are ten feet off the ground.

A player might argue about a call, if the ball was in or out of bounds, but never argues about "Why is the line here?" or "Shouldn't it be another two feet away?" Your children should know what is out of bounds. The boundaries must be clearly communicated and consistent.

When you have small children, you'll have different types of boundaries and rules. When my children were toddlers, one of our house rules was "No jumping on furniture." Well, let me tell you a story about someone breaking one of our house rules.

Enforcing Boundaries with Other Children

My wife and I had been married for a few years and were the proud parents of a bouncing baby boy. Babies are one thing that will get your neighbors talking to you, even if they didn't talk to you before. A couple that lived a few doors away from our home was kind enough to call and see if they could come by and see our son. We scheduled a date and the couple came by with their two small children. The baby's crib was in our bedroom along with a couch. We were gathered in the bedroom, playing with my son and talking to the neighbors when their three-year-old son started running around the room.

I watched this three-year-old sprint back and forth around the couch at breakneck speed, and I was concerned that he might fall and hurt himself. I waited a minute, then another, because I *knew* that one of his parents would stop him at any time. Wrong! How could they let him run around like this? Couldn't they see that this was dangerous? The young sprinter was spinning around the couch when I could no longer contain myself.

I stooped down on my knees and grabbed little Gregory around the waist, in a nice but firm way. "Gregory, we don't run like that in our house," I said. He looked at me and then back at his parents who looked slightly stunned. "OK," was his reply, and he slowly walked around the couch.

My wife, Gregory's parents and I were all playing with my son when a new sound came from behind the couch.

"Wheee … Wheee …"

After slowly spinning my head around as if I were in the *Exorcist*, I couldn't believe my eyes—Gregory was jumping up and down on *my* bed. Was this my imagination, or was this three-year-old actually jumping up and down on my bed as his parents sat next to me and said nothing?

"Wheee … Wheee …"

Nope. It wasn't my imagination, and Gregory had gotten another two good jumps on the bed. And still no reaction from his parents.

"Gregory! Stop that right now!" I said harshly, as I sped over to the bed to grab this child one more time. And his parents still hadn't moved or said a word.

"We don't allow jumping on our bed," I told Gregory and his parents. There aren't enough pleasantries on the planet to gloss over the fact that I was a little ticked off. Gregory and his parents left shortly thereafter and they never set foot in my house again.

I had learned a critical lesson. You can't assume other parents are raising their children the way you want your children to be raised, and you can't assume other children know or care about your house rules. It's your house and it's up to you to control the rules. Don't let anyone break your house rules!

Rules Mean You Care

Putting rules and guidelines in place is an important way of showing your child that you care. All children want to know that their parents care about their safety, care about their education and love them unconditionally. There is no better way of showing your child that you care than to provide the framework for their success. Establishing your house rules is showing your child that you care.

> *"Children need limits on their behavior because they feel better and more secure when they live within a certain structure."*
> — DR. LAURENCE STEINBERG

House rules are setting the boundaries. When children don't know where the boundaries are located, they become even more self-centered. Without boundaries, everything is about oneself, which unfortunately fits in nicely with many aspects of our society today. It's all about get-rich-quick, self-gratification and me, me, me. Without rules, your children will probably have a harder time with those things that require work to achieve. A child raised in a home without rules will have a more difficult time conforming to any rules later in life. Sooner or later, there will be rules (also known as laws) that your child will have to adhere to. And if they don't, the places where many adults go that don't play by the rules are called prisons.

As critical as rules are, they are meaningless if they're not clearly communicated. If children are aware of the rules, more often than not, they will abide by the rules. However, the rules have to be clearly established and communicated. The earlier in your child's life that you establish clear rules, the better.

Remember that setting guidelines for your children is a way to show your children that you care about them, and more importantly, that you love them. Don't assume that your children, or any others, automatically know your rules. It's up to you to make the rules known, as well as the ramifications if the rules are broken.

Clearly defined rules will take assumptions out of play. Your child cannot assume something if it's already been clearly stated otherwise. Carl knows that he can't have any friends over if he hasn't cleaned his room. Bryan knows that when his friends come into the house, they must remove their baseball cap. Asia knows that she has to do her homework when she gets home before she can go to a friend's house. The key is for you to establish the guidelines and then enforce them consistently.

Know the Rules

While it is up to you to create the rules in your home, it's best if you can have a family meeting about the rules once your children become of age.

Some children as young as two years old might be included in a family meeting if they have an older sibling, while others might not be able to sit still until three or four. The point is that you should include your children in family meetings as soon as possible.

The value of having a meeting to discuss the rules is that it removes the "I didn't know" factor. It's tough to discipline a child for not following the rules if they can legitimately say they didn't know about the rules. A family meeting to discuss the rules is a good means of open and honest communication. Setting expectations with your house rules is a cornerstone in successfully raising your child.

Discuss the house rules and seek questions from your children to make sure they understand them. There will be cases where your children don't agree with the rules, so you should be open enough to listen to their concerns. Your child may bring forth legitimate issues that you haven't considered, so be smart enough to alter the rules if it makes good sense. Getting your child involved in discussing the rules is also a better way of getting his or her buy-in. While I strongly suggest that you always seek your children's understanding of the rules, don't be foolish enough to think that you'll *always* gain their understanding or their agreement.

Your objective is not to get your child's agreement. Your objective is to make sure that your child is aware of the rules, and preferably, understands the rules. Agreement may or may not occur, and that's alright. While your child can help influence the rules, he or she cannot set them. You set the house rules, not your child. In the words of my father, Isidor Arthur, to his young son (me), "And when you're the parent, you can set the rules."

Know the Consequences

The other part of setting house rules is to clearly define the consequences if a rule is broken. While clearly discussing the rules, you must also discuss what happens if one is broken. In life, actions have consequences. You'll be teaching your child a valuable lesson when they understand that their choices in life will have consequences. So when a rule is broken, disciplinary action may come into play. If your children have been involved in establishing the rules, they should also be involved in setting the disciplinary actions associated with the rule. Since both the rule and the associated discipline were both determined before the rule was broken, there shouldn't be any conflict about the disciplinary action.

There are far too many variations of breaking a rule to determine the associated consequence for each, but suffice it to say that the punishment should fit the crime. So if your child bites another child, the punishment for that action would be quite different than if your child forgets to turn in a homework assignment. You can set general guidelines for punishment, but you'll have to use *your good judgment* to make sure the punishment fits the infraction.

Let's say that your nine-year-old son, Harold, comes home with a report card with C's in every subject. If he came home and thought those grades are OK, then you probably haven't managed Harold's expectations. You should have already set the expectation that as long as he tried his best, the grades wouldn't matter. So the question is, "Does straight C's represent his best effort?" Nine out of ten times, the answer is no, because your child is smarter than that. Smart is usually tied to hard work and dedication, and so are grades! Your child will be smarter if you have house rules that set the foundation and the support system for Harold to do his best.

So let's examine what your house rules might look like related to school:

- Harold goes to bed by 9 pm if he has school the next day.
- Harold has a designated place for homework or study *without* a TV.
- Harold has a specific time when he must work on homework and/or study.
- You review Harold's homework on a regular basis.
- Harold eats something for breakfast before going to school.
- Ensure that Harold wakes up in time to properly prepare for school.
- Harold arrives at school on time.

And for extra credit:

- Both parents are involved at school and attend parent-teacher conferences.
- Both parents are involved in raising and disciplining their child.

None of these items is molecular biology material, and each item on its own is no big deal. The power comes from combining all of these small things. The sum is greater than the parts. By combining these items, you've set up a structure and a foundation for Harold to be successful in school.

Become an After-Hours' Educator

The most interesting aspect is that all of these house rules, except the extra credit, are entirely within one parent's control. None of the items above are based on Harold's test scores, behavior, spelling or writing. They're all based on you and factors where you have total control. Harold's success will largely be dependent on you, the structure you've put in place, and your ability to consistently enforce your own rules.

Parents in Asian cultures become "after-hours' educators." It's not just because Asian parents expect their children to get A's in class; they also put the structure in place to support it. Every child in America would be better served if their parents also became after-hours' educators. You'll be well on your way if you put the educational support in place.

If you're a single parent, the rules supporting education don't change. From the list above, only the extra credit rules call for involvement by both parents, so that is out of your *total* control. However, you may have the ability to influence the other parent, since at least for a short time, you got along pretty well. Additionally, since you'll both always be the child's parents, it would be in everybody's best interest if you could participate together. Try to influence the other parent to take part, and if they don't, then let it go. Control what you can control, influence what you can influence, and let the rest go. If you've really tried to influence the other parent and they've decided they don't want to participate, then let it go. You can rest easy knowing that you tried your best and are doing the best *you* can.

Nonetheless, you can still make a difference in your child's life by putting the proper house rules in place to support your child's education. And while there are many things that take money, none is required for the educational house rules. The most important thing is your time and spending it with your child.

Time (Not Money) Is the Key

Let me state that again, in case you didn't catch it: *Money is not the key in raising your children, time is.* In our history, there are thousands of great stories where parents with very little money raised their children to be extremely successful. From CEOs of Fortune 100 companies to United States senators to presidents. Becoming a great teacher may be your child's calling. Or perhaps becoming a scientist or a doctor ... Your child may choose to be a pastor of a church, or live his or her life like many others, trying to do God's will by treating others with kindness and love. Today, your young children can still become anything when they grow up, and it largely depends on you to put them on the right path.

Children will sometimes break the rules and will frequently test the limits. You need to be prepared to say no and mean it, but don't say no too fast. Wait to hear the entire story before you decide to respond to your child. As parents, we often think we know the answer sooner than we do. And even if we do know the answer, let your children finish their thoughts before chopping them off at the knees with a sound no.

The value of waiting is that you might find at the end of the story, that there may be a good reason to change your no to a maybe, or even to a yes. If you often say no and it quickly changes to yes, you're sending your child a strong message:

"Although I might *say* no, I don't *really* mean it." You don't want to send your child the wrong message, and if you do, you'll find your child will slowly begin to manipulate you more and more, just like any child, until the routine and structure in your house is no longer yours. Wait and listen. When you say no, mean it, and stick to it.

Ways to Say No

Here's a good list from Jean Clarke on "Ways to Say No:"

   I.   No
   II.   No, for sure.
   III. No, and that's final.
   IV.   No! Do not ask me again.
   V.   I have thought about it and the answer is no.
   VI.   We don't have money for that right now.
   VII. You already have enough of those.
   VIII. I don't approve of it.
   IX.   Nice try.
   X.   I already know you know how to nag.
   XI.   Go find something else to do.
   XII. I'm starting to get really angry.
   XIII. Your whining makes me think you already have too many toys.
   XIV. I remember saying no.
   XV.   Who is the grown-up here?
   XVI. I'm not going to change my mind about this.
   XVII. It's your money but I'm in charge.

I would suggest you change the way you say no based on the circumstances and use the list above. You'll find it a lot easier to say no when you vary how you say it, and it'll be easier for you to get through to your child that "No means no."

Act Quickly when Rules Are Broken

When rules are broken, and they will be, it is critical that you follow up quickly and discipline your child accordingly. When I was in corporate America, we had a practice of giving employees timely, constructive feedback. I've found that timely, constructive feedback works very well when raising children, too. So, the moment you find out about a house rule being broken, take immediate action. Regardless of your children's height, get eye to eye with them and let them know they broke a rule and why you're taking disciplinary steps.

If it's a toddler, it might be a time out. If it's an older child, it may be no telephone usage. You should never waiver in disciplining your child, as appropriate.

If your child is behaving badly, you must stop the child immediately. No excuses. You may have to remove the child from the situation and this may mean physical intervention. By physical intervention, I mean picking up the child and walking away, or by holding their hand and leading them away. Bad or improper behavior should **never** be tolerated.

Even if you're not home, take appropriate disciplinary action as soon as you can. Explain to your child why the behavior was not appropriate and tell the child how he or she should behave. Try to always offer your child an alternative. Many children haven't thought through appropriate choices, so as a parent, it's your job to offer alternatives to your children and help them make smart choices.

Beware of Clever Children!

Children will also play one parent against the other, or one adult against the next, or whatever they can do to get their way. It's what children do and you better protect yourself against it.

My daughter is a charming, loving child that I love dearly, but she will try to work either her mother or me so that she gets what she wants. *Beware, children can be very clever.*

Here is a typical conversation:

Daughter: "Mom, it's Friday, can I watch TV? I've finished all my homework."

Mom: "If you've finished your homework, I don't mind, but check with your dad."

Daughter: "Dad, I just wanted you to know I'm turning on the TV and Mommy said it was OK since I finished my homework."

So the television goes on with me thinking it was OK with my wife. Well, I guess it really was alright with my wife, but my daughter had conveniently removed the "check with your dad" part while letting her dad know it was OK.

Whether in single-parent homes or in two-parent homes, get in the habit of asking your children if they spoke with their other parent, or grandmother, or uncle, or any other adult in your household before you respond. Children learn at an early age the art of manipulation and will use it to their advantage. Don't let your child manipulate you.

It's Not Too Late

The earlier you have your house rules in place, the better. If children have always had guidelines in the house, you'll find that you will have a much easier time getting through the tough times of parenting. But if you don't have any rules in place, it's not too late to start today.

Based on the age of your child, you'll have to gradually begin implementing your house rules. You don't want to put too many immediate constraints on a child that has ruled your house until now. This goes for all parents whose children run the house, and there are many.

Expect Rules to Change over Time

Recognize that over time, your rules will likely change. One of my house rules that has changed is based on technology. Have you ever had a conversation with someone who was wearing an ear piece for their cell phone, even though they *weren't* on the phone? Wireless technology has many people walking around looking like they should be on *Star Trek*, while in reality they're simply waiting for that next very important phone call.

One day, my nephew came over to my house with his ear piece in his ear. He walked into the house and began having normal conversations with others. After about twenty minutes of interaction, I realized that he wasn't planning on removing his ear piece. Well that was the beginning of a new house rule.

No cell phone ear pieces allowed in the house if you're not on the phone. And if you are, please excuse yourself so no one else is inconvenienced by your conversation. That rule may seem odd to some, but it works well in my home. You should determine what rules work best for you in yours.

How to Get Started

Begin by establishing the three most important rules you need in your home and put them into effect immediately. Explain to your child why you're putting house rules in place—and remember that you must abide by the same rules. After all, it begins with you. Over time, you can put additional rules in place, and you'll start to see a slow transformation in your child.

Think of your undisciplined child as a wild or unbridled horse. The horse wants to run wild and do as it pleases. So does your child. The horse may be the best looking, fastest and smartest stallion ever on God's green earth. But if that horse isn't tamed or bridled, the horse will never become the best horse it can be, and it will never care or know the difference. Neither will your unbridled child.

You may have a child that has the potential to become the next Barack Obama, Oprah Winfrey, Shirley Chisholm or Thurgood Marshall. Your children have the intelligence and drive to become anything they desire, if you put the boundaries and rules in place to let them flourish.

Our streets are filled with young boys and girls with all the potential in the world, and they'll never realize it. Their parents didn't put the rules in place for many of these children to succeed, and therefore, most of them won't. You have a chance to make a *huge* difference in your child's life. Implement the structure and discipline that gives your child a good chance to succeed. Establish your house rules and stick to them. You'll be glad you did.

Take This with You:

- *Children need guidelines, so establish house rules.*
- *Communicate clearly.*
- *Everyone in the house must abide by the rules.*

And Remember:

- *As the parent, you determine the rules.*
- *Set up an educational support structure.*
- *Enforce your rules.*

5
Managing Expectations

Parents have a unique opportunity to show and tell their children what is expected. Children will typically do what's expected of them. That's not the case with adults, but children will usually meet expectations. And that's an area of opportunity for many parents who have low or virtually no expectations of their children. Your child *will* perform to the level of what is expected. If not much is expected, not much will be gained. You've got to set high expectations.

When I was growing up, I didn't have any real expectations of what I wanted to do or be "when I grew up," but my parents did. Most children don't know what they want to do later in life, and it's up to parents to set and manage expectations.

ex-pect   *1: regard as likely*
              2: look for as appropriate or one's due

My neighborhood was all black and I attended an all-black grammar school, but expectations were still high. While in grammar school, I was a pretty good student and never really gave much thought to "what came next." My parents had a plan for me that was easy and simple. After successfully completing a grade in school, the plan was to successfully complete the next grade. So after completing sixth grade, the expectation was that I would go to seventh grade, try my best and go to eighth grade. After that, I would try my best, graduate and go to high school. It was a clear expectation in our home that what came after grammar school was high school. And what came after high school was college. It was no big deal to me, but it was a clear expectation, and no other options ever entered my young, feeble brain. My mother's statement always seemed to ring true, "Try your best and good things happen."

My mother was a secretary in the divinity school at the University of Chicago and she often typed up manuscripts for professors. Like many black families that migrated from the South, we lived on the second floor of a two-flat apartment building with relatives living in the apartment on the first floor. My brother, sister and I were all good students because we really didn't have a choice.

There go those expectations again!

In high school, ninth grade was followed by tenth grade, which was followed by eleventh grade, senior year and graduation. There was never any consideration of not finishing high

school, or of not going to college. My parents had high expectations of me, and they let me know that I would be the first one
in our family to get a college degree. I never thought of it as a
big deal, just what was supposed to happen next. I could still
hang out, have fun and do the things teenage boys did in the
early '70s. It was just that I had to do my best in school along
the way.

My parents also made sure that I was in an environment
that supported their expectations. They made sure I had a quiet
place to study and do my homework, get a good night's sleep,
and get to school on time after eating breakfast.

ex-pec-ta-tions   *1: the act or an instance of expecting or looking*
                       forward
                       2: something expected or hoped for
                       3: the probability of an event

Don't Let Children Make Educational Choices

My parents, Rehova and Isidor, were a couple of pretty
smart parents by the time I was born. Like most first-time
parents, they had to learn along the way, and they learned
very valuable lessons with my older brother. The expectations weren't quite as clear for my brother Byron, and since he
was six years older than me, he had the time, knowledge and
experiences to tell my parents what worked and what didn't
work so well for him. My parents learned that you can't let
children in grammar school make educational choices. They
also learned that if you let high school students make educational decisions, you might not get what you want, and not

necessarily what your high school student really wants—*or* needs. What you get is what your high school student *thinks* he or she wants *at the time.*

Anyway, by the time my brother gave his advice and suggestions to my parents, I didn't have much of a choice. High school comes after junior high and grammar school, and college comes after high school. It was clear that a college diploma was in my future and my parents' expectations were the reason. Not once did I consider anything other than getting a college degree. Expectations drive behavior.

Parental expectations about education, chores, respect and virtually anything can be the "fire in the belly" that drives your son or daughter.

The Consortium on Chicago School Research recently concluded a study of public high school students in Chicago and found that only 6 of 100 high school freshmen will get a college degree and only 3 of 100 black students will get a college degree. Parents can do so much better. That's why we must manage the educational expectations of our children.

man-age   *1: to look after and make decisions about*

2: to make and keep under one's control

3: to treat with care

4: to succeed in one's purpose

Manage Your Child Like a Baseball Player

A key in being a "good" parent is to be a good manager to your child. Manage your child's life like a raw baseball player with loads of untapped talent. As in many sports, some children, like ballplayers, have to be well managed to reach their potential. It's up to you to take responsibility to manage the life, the surroundings and the choices that your child can make. If you don't manage your child's life, it probably won't get managed. And that's the issue with many children whose lives are unmanaged. As a parent, you've got to take responsibility for managing the expectations of your child.

But managing expectations doesn't mean you have to become a control freak. Children should still have the ability to make reasonable choices and you should always maintain veto power; just don't use it too frequently.

By showing your son what a clean room looks like, when you tell him to clean up his room, he knows what is expected. When you say clean up the kitchen, he should know what a clean kitchen looks like. Does that mean

"If you paint in your mind a picture of bright and happy expectations, you put yourself into a condition conducive to your goal."
— NORMAN VINCENT PEALE

only the dishes should be washed? Do you have to put up the dishes after they've been washed? Do you have to wipe off the oven or the countertop? How about the kitchen table? Who has to clean out the pots? You should show your child what a clean kitchen means to you. That way, when you ask if the kitchen is clean, everyone knows the expectations of a clean kitchen. That's how you set expectations.

Managing expectations can even change how your children think.

Set Expectations Early

It's common for young girls to play with dolls, and my daughter was no exception. One day while holding a baby doll, I heard her tell a friend that she wanted to have a baby.

"Have a baby." For some reason, that comment concerned me. In growing up with my sister, Regina, she had lots of dolls in her room and on many occasions played "house" and pretended to have a baby. That didn't make Regina have a baby out of wedlock, but times have changed and my daughter's comment concerned me.

If my sister grew up playing with dolls and never seriously considered having a baby before she got married, maybe it had something to do with the expectations set by my parents. It was a mantra stated to many children through the years: Don't go to jail, finish high school and don't bring any babies home. That was a saying to both boys and girls, and it appears that it worked.

Well, I determined that the time was right to set expectations with my three-year-old daughter when it came to babies.

"Morgan, having babies can be a beautiful thing, but let me tell you what worked for Mommy and Daddy," I told her. "First you have to finish high school, and when you graduate from high school, you go to college. After graduating from college you have to get a job. After getting a job, you get married, and after you get married is when you can have a baby."

"Not everyone is going to do it in that order, and that's OK too, but that's the way Mommy and Daddy did it, and that's the way we'd like you to do it, too."

A couple of years later, a big smile came over my face when I heard my daughter telling a friend as they played with dolls,

"I want to have a baby. But first I have to finish high school. And when I finish high school, I have to finish college. And after I finish college, I'd like to get married. And after I'm married, I can have a baby."

Children want your approval and, if they know you care and you love them, they will seek your approval more often than not. Approval to a child is like a bottle to a baby. Your child would prefer to get approval from you, but if they don't, they'll take it from someone else. So it's important to have high expectations for your child, and when they meet those expectations, show your approval. Children will rise to the level that you set to get your approval.

Raise the Bar

Gaining your approval will typically mean that your child will stay in your good graces and out of trouble. Many parents have kept the expectations of their children too low, and children perform accordingly. Take the "trouble threshold" study for instance.

There was a study of high school students that reflected the "trouble threshold." The trouble threshold is the bar where the high school students would get into trouble at home if they performed below the bar. For the black children surveyed, the trouble threshold was a C–, with a C– being the lowest grade they could receive without getting into trouble at home. And guess what? Those black students performed accordingly and had an average grade of C–.

White students had a trouble threshold of a B–, and performed accordingly and averaged a B–. Asian students had a trouble threshold of an A–, and of course they averaged an A–.

So let's make this point crystal clear, children typically perform to the level that is expected. If your child knows you'll approve B's and C's, you can count on rarely seeing an A. If your child thinks it is alright with you if they skip school sometimes, then they will skip school. If your child thinks it's OK with you if they don't study or do their homework, then they won't study or do their homework. You must set the expectations and provide the structure to support those expectations, and your child will meet or exceed those expectations almost every time.

All three racial groups studied (blacks, whites and Asians) performed at the level that was acceptable without getting into trouble at home. The most discouraging fact is that black students in the study were OK as long as they didn't get D's. The issue is that the parents of these students do not have high enough educational expectations of their children. You can put educational structures in place that support your expectations.

You can have high expectations of your child, even if you weren't the recipient of high expectations yourself. Just because you didn't get A's and B's in school doesn't mean your child can't be an honor role student, if you put the proper structure in place. And while grades may be a measure of success, there is so much more. Success in school might be getting to school on time, participating in class discussions, doing homework, turning in homework on time, and studying. If your child does all of those things, then he or she should be successful. And good grades will come as a by-product of that success.

Seeing the Values Take Root

Not long ago, I overheard a conversation between my son and one of his friends on the telephone. I wasn't on the phone, but was standing just a few feet away and my son hadn't seen me.

"I've got to study a little more," my son said into the phone.

I could only hear my son's response to a female voice.

"My grades are OK, but I need a better grade in chemistry," he said.

There was much more chatter on the other end of the line before my son responded, "I'm not studying for my parents anymore. I'm studying for me. I want the better grade."

Sooner than you think, the values that you've worked to instill in your child will take root. I was quite proud that my son had finally decided that good grades were in *his* best interest. Your son or daughter may or may not have good grades, but if you teach your children that your expectation is that they try their best, you will have a successful student. To have a successful student, you'll need to provide the right type of support.

Parental Support Is Key

An example of good parental support could include a good place to study and do homework without a television on in the background. Set up a specified amount of time that should be spent on homework with your support and involvement. Your involvement should include meeting with your child's teachers to show them that you care about your child's education, and that *you* will support the teacher's efforts.

Funny thing about teachers, they'll always work a little harder with those students whose parents are involved. You want to be one of those parents.

Supporting your child's educational needs also means taking the time to review homework assignments and to be available to discuss the homework, or to answer any questions that your child may have. Once again, you are a critical cog in this exercise, and if you don't come through, there's a good chance your child won't succeed. Some children will succeed in spite of their parents, but that's rare.

Structure is a means of managing expectations. Children yearn for structure, but will fight all night long not to have it. Structure for a young child often comes in the form of putting the foundation in place to support your expectations.

Start Managing Expectations Early

Even when raising an infant, you can begin managing your child's expectations. Structure for an infant could include setting times for eating and sleeping. It may take a newborn baby a few months to get with the program, and then he or she will usually eat and sleep based on the schedule you've set. Setting up eating and sleeping times may not be hard to do, but sometimes it's not so easy. The easy thing might be to pick up your baby in the middle of the night and bring him back to bed with you. That would be the quick, easy fix that can get you into trouble later. If you regularly picked up your child from their crib in the middle of the night when they were crying, you will soon have managed the expectations of your child that you will come and pick him up and take him back to your bed in the middle of the night. I'm not suggesting that you let your child cry all night without your intervention; my point is to make you aware that your actions with your children will drive their expectations.

The most important factor in managing expectations is to spend time with your children so they understand your expectations. Time is your most precious commodity, and you've got to use it wisely. You've got to *make* time to spend with your children so that you can manage their expectations, and putting the required structure in place will be worth the effort. The key is time, not money.

Take, for instance, the issue of potty training your child. Children that are potty trained at an earlier age are typically trained by their parents that fifteen to thirty minutes after eating or drinking, they should sit on the potty. Going to sit on the potty isn't something your child will do naturally. It takes your time to sit your child on the potty and continue to do so until your child has figured it out that he or she should go and sit on the potty at the appropriate time.

Conversely, if you don't start teaching your children about potty training until they're three or four, you've managed your children's expectations that it's alright not to be potty trained until three or four. This will also damage your children's psyche when they realize that their friends know how to go to the bathroom and they don't. It's not a shortcoming of the children, but a shortcoming of the parent.

Parents can manage expectations related to virtually anything: respect, responsibility, behavior, hygiene and education, just to name a few.

re-spect   1: *to feel or show honor or esteem for; hold in high*
              regard
              2. *to show consideration for*

Respect Must Be Earned

Respect is something that parents often expect from their children and sometimes don't receive. Respect must be earned. You should be respectful of your children if you are to receive respect. Respect is not one of those things that you can demand and get just because you're the parent. It sometimes seems that parents only like half of the equation, and don't take the time to be respectful of their children. Remember that any real change must begin with you, and having a respectful relationship with your children is based on your actions.

Being respectful of your children does not mean that they can speak to you anyway they like. Being a responsible parent also doesn't give you the inherent right to speak to your children in anyway that *you* choose. It is not alright to scream at your children just because they've done something wrong. Try to utilize the "Golden Rule" and attempt to speak to your children in the same manner in which you'd like someone to speak to you. Screaming means nothing more than the fact that you have lost control.

"Where's the Handle?"

When I was growing up, we couldn't answer my parents in any way we chose. At an early age, I was taught that when responding to my parents, an appropriate response was "yes ma'am" or "no sir." We couldn't respond with just a yes or a no.

If we happened to forget, my father would quickly ask, "Where's the handle?" which meant to add ma'am or sir to the response.

I asked my father why he thought it was so important and he told me, "Mo, children have a way of sometimes forgetting who they're talking to and it's hard to say, 'Yeah, ma'am' or, 'What, sir?' Some people would have you think it's a black-white thing, or something associated with slavery, but it's not. It's just a matter of respect, nothing more and nothing less."

So my brother, sister and I grew up always responding to our parents *and* other elders with the appropriate no ma'am or yes sir. Today, I often say yes sir or no ma'am to others and I often get a strange look, since often they're younger than me. I often respond to my children with the same—yes sir, or no ma'am. It has nothing to do with age from my perspective, as my daddy said, "It's just a matter of respect."

Know What's in Your Child's Room

Respect for your children means you'll respect their rights as an individual. Respect *doesn't* mean that you shouldn't go through your children's room unannounced to see what you'll find. It's your job as a parent to know what's going on with your children, and what better way to do this than by going through their room on occasion? It's OK to snoop, and snooping *is not* disrespectful. This probably isn't the politically correct way of being a parent, but it works. And let your children know what to expect; that you may at anytime go through their room. You are responsible for your child and your child's actions for at least eighteen years. You should have an idea if your child has fifteen guns stashed away in his or her room.

"Well, how was I to know that little John had nine rifles in his closet and six handguns in his dresser drawer?"

Or,

"I never go in Stephanie's room. I don't want to invade her privacy. She always closes the door when she goes into her room."

These kind of parents are nuts! As a responsible parent, you need to know what's going on in your child's bedroom. Let your child know you reserve the right to go through their room at any time. By telling your child, you will be managing their expectations. Your children should expect you to go through their room every once in a while, and you should. Lots of things can happen with children in their bedrooms, alone with a TV, or on the Internet.

re-spon-si-bil-i-ty   *1: condition, quality, fact, or instance of being responsible*
2: obligation, accountability, dependability, etc.

Responsibility is a critical component that you should always expect from your children, and your son or daughter should know that they will be responsible for their actions and that actions have consequences. It's a good idea to tell your children that they will be held responsible for their actions, or their lack of taking action. Some would have you think that because they didn't take any action that they had "done nothing wrong." Well, sometimes doing nothing is definitely the wrong answer.

re-spon-si-ble   1: *being the one who must answer or account for
something*
2: *being the cause of explanation*
3: *able to choose for oneself between right and wrong*
4: *able to meet one's obligations: trustworthy,
reliable*

Staying in a burning house and sitting in your bedroom with no action may get you killed. Action is required, and doing nothing is not acceptable. When you hear someone say something about someone in a way that does not represent how you feel, you should speak up. No action means staying silent, and that first comment, while it may only be one person's opinion, may come across as a fact. Not taking action is a choice. Just as responsibility is a choice.

Teaching Responsibility

You can make sure that your child, at the appropriate age, has responsibility for some household chores. At a very early age, teach your children to put away their toys when they've finished playing. In so doing, you are teaching them to be responsible for putting away things after they've used them. Make your children responsible for taking out the garbage or cleaning up their rooms or washing the dishes. It's important that your children have an appropriate role in household chores, and understand that it is expected that they will perform their duties. Hopefully at a later age, you might not even have to remind them of their chores, but we're not seeking perfection.

Don't let your children off the hook by determining that they're too young for housework, or that you can do it all. As a toddler, your child should have some responsibility in putting away their toys and helping you make the bed. You want your children to be responsible for their behavior, responsible for their hygiene, responsible for doing their best and responsible for giving thanks. Very few things are as important as teaching your child responsibility. And remember, you'll have to be a responsible adult to raise a responsible child. It all begins with you, but the beauty of it is that it doesn't end there. You can teach your child a life lesson about responsibility that may be passed on for generations and make a difference in many lives long after you're gone. You can make a difference that can impact generations, so don't miss your chance.

Effort Counts More than Grades or Winning

Based on the great parents with whom I was blessed, I've always told my children that their best effort was more important to me than good grades or winning a baseball game. Not that I don't want to win a baseball game as much (probably more) as anyone, or that we tolerate bad grades from our children. Grades only tell one piece of the story, and you need to take into account your child's effort.

Stress success with your child. For some children, success might be an A in one subject and a C in another. Success is trying their best.

As a coach of a youth baseball team, it became clear to me that often parents mismanage expectations. When coaching tee ball the previous year, it was nice that all parents cheered for both teams. Tee ball is where the players hit the ball off a tee, rather than hitting a pitched baseball. The games were sometimes slow, but parents from both teams actually showed excellent sportsmanship. Naturally, parents wanted their team to win, but the key was for the children to have fun and learn fundamental baseball.

The next year with pitched balls, it seemed the rules suddenly changed. The coaches seemed to be much more driven about winning, and so the players became much more fixated on winning the game, too. Soon those same parents that were rooting for both teams a year ago, weren't too pleased when a member of the opposing team made a good play. They screamed at the umpires and got caught up in winning the game. To no one's surprise, you would often see young boys crying because their team didn't win. Sometimes the parents were crying too. Somewhere along the way, it appeared that in order to be successful you had to win. That's simply not true.

Success may mean winning a game, but your child's success should not be based on winning a game or getting an A in a class. Success should be managed as an expectation. John Wooden, the legendary coach of UCLA had a great philosophy about success versus winning. Success in a Wooden-coached basketball game meant that the team ran the plays as they had in practice. Success was playing good aggressive defense, rebounding, and blocking out. Success was taking the open shot. Success for those UCLA basketball teams included all the above. If the team did all those things, then the team was successful and would *usually* score more points than the opponent and win the game. But the team could achieve success and still *not* win the game.

In the NCAA basketball tournament, sixty-five teams start the tournament and all but one of those teams lose their final game. Losing that last game to those sixty-four teams doesn't mean their season wasn't a success, it only means another team scored more points in a particular game.

Success shouldn't mean winning, particularly in children. Success to your children should be doing their best and that should be based on expectations you've set. You can shape what success looks like for your child, and in doing so, you'll be managing their expectations.

Excellence Is a Habit

Managing expectations is also a great way to drive good habits. You can teach your children good habits for controlling their emotions. Finding a quiet space for your children as a means of controlling their temper or anger will serve both of you well. Setting up good habits at a very early age will make it so much easier for your children, and easier for you to catch a pattern that you can address. Much of the success your children will have will be based on their habits. Studying, manners, and many virtues are based on habits. Excellence is nothing more than a habit, and expectations drive habits.

Take This with You:

- *Set high expectations.*
- *Children want to please.*
- *Define success.*

And Remember:

- *Manage the expectations.*
- *Expect good things.*
- *Determine your child's habits.*

6
Attitude Is Everything

There is a good chance that your attitude will determine your life. More importantly, your attitude will impact your child, for better or for worse. Positive thinking is an attitude, and so is confidence.

at-ti-tude *1: A position of the body or manner of carrying oneself, indicative of a mood or condition*
2: A state of mind or feeling with regard to some matter

Four years ago, my family opted to try something a little different. We decided to drive to Sun Valley ski resort for a couple of days after visiting my sister-in-law in Boise, Idaho.

Life Lesson on the Ski Slope

Going skiing was a big deal for us, and this would be both of my children's first time skiing. My son was thirteen at the time, and my daughter was nine. I had skied a couple of times while in high school, and a few times while in Denver. If you haven't seen the Rocky Mountains, they are truly one of nature's treasures. My wife had skied a couple of times, and certainly preferred the spa over the slopes. But we all agreed it would be a nice family trip.

Like most first-time skiers, my children signed up for ski lessons. Both children took to skiing like a duck to water. After four hours of excellent ski lessons from one of the pros, the children were very confident and self-assured on the slopes. Near the end of our two-day trip, both children became slightly more daring and started skiing more difficult ski runs.

The sun was setting in the mountains and it was the first and only time that I had actually seen "purple mountain majesties." The sun's rays on the snow-covered mountain tops made the mountains look purple. For a boy from the Midwest, it was a most amazing sight.

My daughter started getting cold and decided to join her mother in the ski lodge. My son and I decided to take one last run, and we opted to take a run we hadn't skied before. My son's confidence was sky high and he had fallen only once or twice earlier in the day. As we took the chairlift up the mountain, you could see the purple mountains. They were inspiring.

As we got off the ski lift, it was clear to see that the entire mountain looked different from our top-of-the-hill vantage point. Skiing over to the beginners' run, the slopes had an eerie feeling. It wasn't dark yet, but the hues from the clouds and the sun gave the mountain a different feeling. Looking down the ski run, it was hard to tell the difference between a slight incline and a steep slope and it looked very strange.

Slowly, we began our descent, and it was really hard to see the variations of the snow on the hill. The actual skiing wasn't harder, but because we couldn't see the slopes very well, it felt much harder. I looked over at my son and he had a look of concern on his face. Ten minutes ago, he had skied a similar run and was one of the most confident beginners on the slopes. That look of confidence had been replaced with one of doubt and fear.

A moment later, my son took a fall. It wasn't a tough fall, and it was a move that ten minutes earlier he had done with ease. The mountain looked spooky, though, and I thought it would be perfect for a scene in *The Twilight Zone*.

"Get up," I yelled as I continued just a little farther down the hill.

"I can't," he screamed back at me.

I stopped suddenly and looked back up the hill where my son was flipping around on his side like a fish out of water. After a couple of attempts, he was back up on his skis. Four or five feet later, though, he fell again. This time, I didn't say a word.

"I can't get up," he hollered again. "My skis are broken."

With that comment, I slowly began my way back up the hill. When you're sidestepping up a mountain, it may take you five minutes to go fifty feet. By the time I got back up to him, he had stopped flopping around and was lying on his side, defeated.

"Can you get up?" I asked.

"No, my ski is broken," was his reply.

Finally, I helped him to his feet and he declared, "I'm taking my skis off and walking down the mountain, my ski is broken."

"Oh, no you're not," was my sharp response. "Do you know how long it would take to walk down this mountain? The temperature is dropping and it would take us a very long time to walk down, probably thirty to forty minutes. Besides, I'm not so sure that your ski is broken. Let me check out your skis!"

Before I took a look at the skis, I started laughing. I couldn't help myself. My wife says I laugh at the strangest things and she's right. My son gave me a very mean look.

As I looked at the skis, which were fine as I suspected, I asked my son, "You know what's broken, don't you?" I laughed.

There was no reply.

My laughter hadn't stopped as I repeated, "You know what's broken don't you? It's your mind. You've been skiing the last couple of days without a problem. With the sun setting, the slopes looked spooky to me, too. I understand that it feels kind of scary, but I know together we can ski down the mountain and be in the lodge in ten minutes. I know you can do it. The problem is only in your mind, so let me help you and let's take it nice and slow."

With that statement, I received a pissed-off look from a very displeased thirteen-year-old. I knew he was not happy with my laughing, and I apologized.

My son got back up on his skis and we started down the hill very slowly. The slopes still had an eerie feeling. We skied first to the left, then to the right, very slowly. After about ten seconds without a fall, I gave a few encouraging comments, "See, you can do it, we'll just take it nice and slow."

After a minute or so, I could sense a touch of confidence as my son suggested that we go a little faster. Soon, we picked up a little more speed and within a minute, we were making our way down the slopes as we had earlier in the day. The look of desperation and fear was gone and had been replaced with a look of confidence once again. Within fifteen minutes, we were back in the ski lodge.

> *"Whether you think you can or think you can't—you are right."*
> —HENRY FORD

What had occurred on the ski slopes was a life lesson and I took the time in the ski lodge to make sure my son understood the lesson. We got a good laugh out of the experience, since once again he had regained his confidence.

My son is a pretty confident young man, and in areas where he has a good foundation, his confidence will sustain him in bad times. When it came to skiing with a one-day foundation, his confidence was shaky, and it took only one bad scenario for him to lose all confidence.

Your child will have confidence in those areas where you have built a strong foundation. If the foundation is weak, a small fall can turn into a massive loss of confidence. That lack of confidence could be in reading, baseball or virtually anything else. The biggest loss of confidence could be in one's self. Controlling your attitude can enhance your confidence.

Use Change to Your Advantage

One of the most valuable assets you have as a human being on God's green earth is that you have the ability to change. You have the ability to change your attitude and you can modify virtually any habit. There aren't too many other living things that can choose to change a habit, but you can.

Since the mind is so incredible and powerful, use it to your advantage. A positive attitude can provide you with the ability to change how you see your life and that of your child. Have a positive attitude about the opportunity to get smarter when things go wrong. Have a positive vision for the future of your children. If you don't have a vision for your children, then any road can get them there. Often those roads won't include education, because the easy streets usually don't.

And to think, we only utilize about 10 percent of the brain's capability. Most of our vital functions would probably just shut down if they were underutilized by 90 percent. But not the brain. The brain just idles along at a lowly 10 percent clip, and that's normal. One could make a pretty good argument that most of us are underachievers, and we could rise well above the norm if we utilized our brain just a little more. Controlling your attitude is nothing more than a brain exercise. Positive thinking or optimism is an attitude. Confidence is an attitude.

Build Confidence in Your Child

Everyone is born with some level of confidence. It's just that confidence is like a little light shining that parents have the ability to turn into a floodlight or diminish entirely. Confidence must be powered up by parents or others in a child's life at a fairly young age. Unfortunately there are many children with little lights of confidence that haven't been turned up at all. Thank goodness for small favors, since that means at least they still have some confidence; it's just that it hasn't been touched by their parents. Build the foundation in your children to make their confident light shine bright.

One of the best ways to brighten your children's light is to cultivate their attitude with confidence, and a good way to do this is through education. For young children, a great way to get started is through early childhood education. I'm speaking of the education before kindergarten that will build confidence in your child.

Your child has the ability to read long before kindergarten, as well as the capability to understand basic math and geography. A child exposed to educational materials at an early age will have more confidence in his or her abilities. You can help build that confidence by having your child involved in educational programs *before* kindergarten. The program could be a formal one, or a program custom-designed by *you* with some help from your local library.

Giving your children the benefit of early education will provide a great foundation for their life. An educational foundation will also provide your children with something that is more precious than gold—inner confidence. Confidence is an attitude.

The Power of Positive Thinking

Another way to improve your attitude is to focus on the positive. The positive must start first in your mind. You have the ability to picture things in your mind that haven't happened yet. It doesn't have anything to do with what's standing before you, but what you can envision in your mind.

Positive thinking is a habit. A positive outlook on life is nothing more than having the right kind of attitude.

> *"The greatest discovery of any generation is that a human being can alter his life by altering his attitude."*
> — WILLIAM JAMES

Many athletes are known to use the power of positive thinking to envision what they'd like to see happen. In football, this could be making a critical tackle on an important play, or getting a key hit during a rally in baseball, or hitting the free throw in basketball to tie the game. Seeing things in a positive way in your mind's eye is critical to your success.

In high school, I had a friend who always focused on the positive, and it proved to be a great lesson. David was always one of the most well-liked guys in high school, and he had a charm about him that was compelling. While not the best looking, or the best athlete, or the smartest (well, he might have been one of the smartest), David had a gift for finding something good to say about anybody.

While I grew up under the guidelines of "If you can't say anything nice, don't say anything," David's motto seemed to be "If you can't say anything nice, then look harder and find something nice you can say, but only if you mean it."

I remember when a couple of girls were walking toward school and David and I were sitting on the stairs. I was thinking,

"Alexis doesn't look real good in that green dress," and out of David's mouth came, "Alexis, I really like those shoes."

"Those shoes?" I thought. I had never looked at her shoes, and David was right, I liked her shoes, too. Alexis was smiling from ear-to-ear. In fact, I found out later that Alexis hadn't been feeling good and David's comments had made her day.

Sometimes it was their hair, sometimes their earrings, or nails, or dress, or purse, and sometimes their smile, but David could always find something that he liked about anyone. So what if that anyone was usually a female. You get the point; you can really find something nice to say to almost everybody. A kind word can often lift spirits, and one of those spirits might even be yours.

> *"To succeed, we must first believe that we can."*
> — *Michael Korda*

Catch Your Child Doing Something Right

Saying something positive to someone will lift your spirits, and using positive words will also help your attitude. Catch your child doing something the right way and give appropriate praise. It's always better to praise rather than to scold. Count the times you find yourself praising versus scolding. You'll quickly see if you're on the right track. Your words have power. It's important to use positive words when communicating with children.

Find the positive energy in every situation. It becomes so easy to get caught up in what's wrong, rather than in what's right. Something positive can come from almost every situation. The key is for you to find it, and with the proper attitude, you can.

Look Past the Messenger

While looking for a new church home, I bounced around and listened to many sermons from many ministers. Some of the sermons I found quite compelling, while others I found lacked a good message. In speaking with my cousin, Dolores, she told me that she previously had the same problem until she realized the need to look past the messenger in order to receive the message.

With a background in sales and marketing, I found that I was probably being too critical of some of the ministers. Having taken corporate classes in public speaking and making presentations, I sometimes "tuned out" if the minister didn't speak quite right, or if his sermon seemed unorganized. And if the minister said something that I just thought was wrong in the beginning of a sermon, I'd tune him out in a heartbeat.

My tuning out probably caused me to miss some very good sermons because I didn't have the right attitude. Some of the best messages I've received from the pulpit have been lessons that I previously would never have received if I continued to focus on the negative.

Stay Positive

Focus on the positive with your children; not just on the wrong stuff. A positive attitude is within your control. There's an old saying about life being 10 percent what happens to you and 90 percent how you react to it. If you control your reactions and your attitude, your child will reap the lifelong benefits. Find the positive energy in any situation and use it to your advantage. You have control of your mind and you can control your attitude.

In taking responsibility for your reactions and your attitude, you'll find space for growth. When something goes wrong, don't beat yourself up inside. Look at the situation as an opportunity to get smarter. Look at the situation as an opportunity to learn, not to make the same mistake twice.

Everyday is special, so start today; you have the ability to choose your attitude.

Take This with You:

- *Build an educational foundation.*
- *Confidence is an attitude.*
- *Focus on the positive.*

And Remember:

- *Involve your child in a preschool program.*
- *Use positive words.*
- *Choose your attitude.*

7
Reading

Reading will significantly enhance your child's chances of success. Reading is the great equalizer and can put *you* on the same level with just about anybody, anywhere. Reading can take you places you'll never go and help you see things you've never seen before. Reading can educate the uneducated.

read
1: *To comprehend or take in the meaning of something written or printed*
2: *To utter or render aloud something written or printed*

Reading Is Contagious

When I was growing up, we had only one car and one driver in our home. This was fairly common at that time. My mother never drove and my father was the only driver in the house. If you thought the fact that my mother didn't drive stopped her from getting around, you would be wrong.

My father, served as the chauffeur for the entire family, and particularly for my mother. Mommy got around town much more than most of her friends that drove, because my dad would take her everywhere and seemingly never complained. Daddy could chauffeur Mommy for hours at a time and not complain because he *always* had a book. He never went anywhere without a book! Daddy viewed driving his wife anywhere, waiting for her (there were no cell phones) and driving her home as an opportunity. Waiting for his wife was an opportunity for Daddy to read and to get smarter.

While my father only had a high school education, he was one of the smartest men you could ever meet. Daddy got much smarter because he loved to read, read, read. Mommy worked for the University of Chicago and Daddy took pleasure in conversing with the many professors that he met at the university. Many of these professors had multiple advanced degrees, so they often had many letters after their names. Daddy could hold a conversation with any of these professors, some of whom were world renowned, on just about any subject. While my father loved to read, he only read non-fiction.

The philosophy of my father was based on the old saying, "The idle mind is the devil's workshop." Reading was Daddy's way of having an active mind and he learned to enjoy reading. His way of thinking was: 1) reading was a good way to keep your mind active, 2) you can read and be entertained, and 3) if you can read, be entertained *and* learn something at the same time, that's heavenly.

Daddy's reading was contagious. If we were in the car and we knew we would be waiting for my mother, my father made it our responsibility to entertain ourselves, and my sister and I did. Sometimes we entertained ourselves by counting the number of doodle-bugs (Volkswagen Beetles) around the college campus, and the rest of the time we'd entertain ourselves with a book.

Parents who read often have children that read, and this is a huge area of opportunity for parents. Far too many parents aren't reading and neither are their children. Because my father was a reader, I became a reader.

> *"Reading is to the mind what exercise is to the body."*
> — *Joseph Addison*

It had nothing to do with smarts. And because I'm a reader, my son and daughter are avid readers, too.

While I'm not quite the non-fiction reader that my father was, I enjoy reading immensely. In my first years out of college, I read primarily fiction. I had to make it a point to make sure that every third book that I read was non-fiction. With my father as a role model, I had to get some non-fiction books under my belt. It doesn't matter if it's fact (non-fiction) or fiction, the key is to read.

Read with Your Child Every Day

The lack of reading skills is causing black children to fall further behind in school. Studies have shown a linkage between the number of books in a home and reading scores; and white kindergartners have twice the number of books at home versus black kindergartners.

Black kindergartners, on average, start academically behind their white counterparts. If you start out behind someone, given the same course and speed, you'll end up behind them. So black kindergartners are starting out behind white kindergartners and will typically fall further behind throughout high school.

> *"Our minds are lazier than our bodies."*
> — *DUC DE LA ROCHEFOUCAULD*

In 2004, less than 35 percent of black children met national reading guidelines. At the same time, 74 percent of white children met the same guidelines. While there may be some issues with the testing process, let's not make an excuse and pretend the issue is largely the testing process. We've got to improve the reading of black children, and here is something you can do to get started.

Be a role model for your child. That means *you* should read, not just require your child to read. Have a family reading time and your child will enjoy it. Read to your child, beginning in the womb and continue reading to your child until your child can read on his or her own. Then family reading time becomes a time when everyone is reading their own books and not just you reading to your child. Have your child keep a reading journal once they can read. The journal should include at least the title of the book and the author. Other entries could include the number of pages, type of book and comments about the book. Let your child determine what they'd like to include beyond the title and author, since it is their journal.

Setting a Good Example

It was a cold blustery day for getting a car wash, but I was getting a car wash anyway. Since all the seats outside were in the cold, I decided to sit in a small, little-used waiting area. Seated across from me were a young mom and her son who had to be no more than twelve years old. I've been in many car washes, but what I saw when I looked at the young lady and her son was something I hadn't seen in decades.

The young mom was waiting in the sitting room for her car and was holding a book while her son read *out loud to her!* What a great feeling.

Her son was reading out of a book that was clearly above his grade level. Slowly but confidently, he read paragraph after paragraph. On occasion he stumbled with a word and his mother helped him with the word and he continued reading. The young mother probably sensed that I was looking at her and looked up and smiled. I returned the smile and was considering how I could tell the young lady how proud it made me to see her son reading to her.

> *"Reading is a means of thinking with another person's mind; it forces you to stretch your own."*
> — CHARLES SCRIBNER

Before I could say a word, a knock on the glass door notified the young lady that her car was ready.

"Darn," I thought. I really wanted to talk to the young mom, because she was setting such a great foundation for her son, and I wanted to tell her.

The young lady looked at me and I looked at her. It seemed as if she didn't want to leave and I didn't really want her to leave. The man knocked on the glass door again and she slowly got up with her son to leave.

"Excuse me," I said. "I just wanted you to know how impressed I was with your son's reading. That's great!"

> *"The man who does not read good books has no advantage over the man who can't read them."*
>
> *— MARK TWAIN*

"Well, thank you," she said. "I always make sure he reads to me. He's always reading and he reads out loud to me when he's reading harder books. I know how important it is that he read."

"Young man," I said as I looked eye-to-eye with her son. "You are one lucky guy to have a mother like yours. Your mom is right, reading is important. Listen to your mother and keep reading. You can be anything you want to be."

The young mom beamed with pride as she and her son gave me one of the biggest, happiest smiles I had ever seen.

"Thanks so much," she said as they left the waiting room.

I couldn't contain my smile. My heart hadn't been touched like that in quite a while.

How to Get Started

If you're not currently a reader and would like to become one, here are a few suggestions to get you started;

- Go to your local library and get a library card. While you're there, ask about any reading programs; or set a goal to read a book every two or three weeks.
- Determine a subject of interest to you, and read a book on that subject.
- Find a place that you would like to learn about or visit, and read a book about that place.
- Consider something that you would like to learn to do, read a book on it and try to do it.
- Have a family reading time without the television.

And if you need assistance with your reading skills, seek out a literacy program at a library near you. The key is to find something to read that is interesting to you. More important than what you read is *that* you read!

Before you know it, you'll discover all kinds of things that *you* wanted to know, and that's only the beginning. Your child will become a reader with you as a role model. Reading can give you hope. Reading gives you the ability to learn. Reading is one of the most precious gifts that you can give your child.

Take This with You:

- *Reading gives you the ability to continuously learn.*
- *Reading can give you hope.*
- *Reading is about you.*

And Remember:

- *Get your child a library card and use the library.*
- *Establish a family reading hour.*
- *Read every day.*

8
Happiness

hap-pi-ness   *1: state of well-being characterized by emotions
ranging from contentment to intense joy
2: emotions experienced when in a state of
well-being.*

Growing up on the south side of Chicago, I felt I lived in one of the happiest houses on the block. It didn't take long to figure out that ours was one of the happiest families, not only on the block, but of anyone I knew. Sure, my spectrum of people and families wasn't that big, but that didn't matter.

When you're growing up, you get to see lots of little things in other people's homes. As a young child, you get the chance to run in and out of your friends' houses, and you get to see what's going on anytime you run in, or out. Various states of discipline were easy to see; if we could literally *run* in the house, then there typically wasn't much discipline. You certainly found out quickly if you couldn't *run* in the house. Some houses, you could even slam the door. That would never happen in our house.

Not that it happened often, but sometimes you would hear arguments in full steam, some mothers hollering at fathers, some fathers screaming at mothers, and some brothers yelling at their sisters. You could tell the happier houses from the other ones. Sometimes it may have been because the house seemed too strict. Or was it because the living room and dining room were literally roped off (yes, with a rope)? Or was it the tone of voice you usually heard as you were grabbing a cookie and heading back to the alley to play softball?

I knew it wasn't because of the plastic on the living room furniture, because almost *everybody* had plastic on their furniture. I didn't know exactly what it was, but you could *feel* happiness in a home. I felt happy in my house and most of my friends did, too.

In the twenty-nine years that I was blessed with both my parents, and the more than twenty years that I lived under their roof, there was only one time that I heard my parents raise their voices to each other. My parents were happy people and theirs was a happy home. You can make yours a happy home, too.

Money Won't Guarantee Happiness

My father once told me that "Your mother and I may not have as much money as a lot of people, but you won't find a happier couple." For a young boy, that was a lasting impression. So you *could* be happy without a lot of money. Money is often a big driver in everyone's life, but once you get past the necessities, there is little correlation between how much money you have and how much happiness.

Time magazine had an article on *The Science of Happiness,* and I found their findings to be right in line with my parents and their philosophy. The article referenced three components of happiness: pleasure, engagement and meaning. Other keys to happiness that were cited were to be giving, thankful and kind. The latter traits can all be linked to engagement and are much more actionable to me, so I wanted to expand the thought and hopefully make them more meaningful to you. While my parents didn't articulate the findings in the same way as the magazine, they certainly lived their lives accordingly, and as one of their children, I reaped the benefits. Your children will too!

> *"Don't wait around for other people to be happy for you. Any happiness you get you've got to make yourself."*
> — ALICE WALKER

Be Giving

Giving is one of those words that you can use ten different ways.

give   1: to make a present of
            2: to deliver
            3: to place in the hands of
            4: to convey

5: *to bestow*

6: *to grant*

7: *to expose*

8: *to designate*

9: *to sacrifice*

10: *to donate*

> **"If you want
> to lift yourself
> up, lift up
> someone else."**
>
> — BOOKER T.
> WASHINGTON

In showing your child that you are giving, you'll be going beyond the hype. Not only do you believe in giving, you are giving in your lifestyle. Giving doesn't necessarily mean giving a birthday gift on birthdays. It means giving of your time when your child needs to talk, or giving of your time to attend parent-teacher conferences, or giving of your time to be attentive to those you love and those that love you. Giving is a valuable trait. Think of giving as a donation. It could be a donation of your time, energy or effort. The donation could be money, but let's get beyond that! And while the financial donations are great, and you should give what you can, the other donations are more valuable. Volunteering to work at a church function or doing charitable work will give your life more meaning. Volunteering will also give your child a chance to see that you can help others—others that you don't even know. Volunteer work is one of the best ways to demonstrate giving.

My mother was one that always gave of herself. If you needed a place to stay while going through hard times, you could always stay at our house while you got yourself together. Over the years, many people lived with us for a short time, including friends of mine, my brother and my sister. Sometimes having another adult stay at our house meant I had to give up my bedroom so the guest could have a bedroom, and it wasn't a big deal. You see, sometimes my mother gave of her family, too. It was no big deal, because that was how I was raised.

Being a member of the Dorcas Missionary Group at West Point Baptist Church meant my mother was often running around the city visiting the sick or shut-ins. She was chauffeured all over the city by another Dorcas member, or more frequently, by my father. This volunteer work clearly made my mother happy. The giving of your time to others will make you a happier person, too.

Volunteer to help an organization that you'd like to support. Work at your place of worship and reach out to help others. If you live in a giving environment, you'll be showing your child one of life's great lessons. Furthermore, you'll be taking the first of three steps to make yours a happier home.

Be Thankful

thank   1: *to express gratitude, appreciation or acknowledgement to*
2: *a grateful feeling or acknowledgement of a benefit, favor, or the like, expressed by words or otherwise*

In today's society, we take so many things for granted. We all have so much for which to be thankful. One could be thankful for health, thankful for food, thankful for family, or thankful for waking up this morning. While all of the things in your life probably aren't going right, regardless of your current space in life, you have many blessings. It's just that sometimes we get caught up in other things and we can't see or appreciate these blessings.

Many people have a tendency to focus on what's wrong in their lives, rather than on what's right. If eight things go right for you today and two things go wrong, most will focus on the 20 percent that went wrong. Life is what you make it, and focusing on the good will always outshine the bad.

People can give thanks in many ways. A prayer can be a means of giving thanks. Blessing your food before each meal is another means of giving thanks. Being thankful is a critical way of accentuating the positive. Giving thanks will increase your optimism and can change how you see things in life. So, once again, how you see things in life can change your life and the life of your child.

Consider being thankful for the trees and nature's beauty. Consider being thankful for the ability to touch and be touched. Consider being thankful for the many joys of living. Be thankful for wherever you are in life, and also be thankful for the ability to change.

It will be extremely hard to teach your child how to be thankful if you're not thankful. Yes, it begins with you! Teaching your child to pray is a good place to start. Be thankful and pray, your child is watching.

Show Kindness

Being kind is a trait that is truly difficult to teach your child if they have not observed kindness in *your* actions. It's always better to show a child, rather than telling a child. And better than showing your child is involving the child. In my opinion, it's harder to teach kindness because kindness is never about you.

kind-ness   1: *of a friendly, generous, or warm-hearted nature*
                   2: *showing sympathy or understanding*

> *"Kindness is more than deeds. It is an attitude, an expression, a look, a touch. It is anything that lifts another person."*
> — C. Neil Strait

Kindness is a trait that you can live everyday and you won't have a specific time or a place where you can remember to show it. While you may have the ability to put a process in place to regularly show some form of giving and thanks, you can't do the same with kindness. Kindness is more fluid and not as easy to put into a process. Kindness must come from the heart.

Acts of kindness can come at any time or any place. You'll get many opportunities to show kindness in this wacky world in which we live. I recall the first time I heard of the term "random acts of kindness." The thought of random acts of kindness still warms my heart.

In researching kindness, I found the Random Acts of Kindness Foundation at *www.actsofkindness.org*. Their website listed the following ten ideas for kindness:

1) Say hello.
2) Visit a friend.
3) Let another go first.
4) Forgive mistakes.
5) Share a smile.
6) Say hello.
7) Lend a hand.
8) Be tolerant.
9) Offer a hug.
10) Do an act of kindness every day.

> *"Happiness is not achieved by the conscious pursuit of happiness; it is generally the by-product of other activities."*
> — ALDOUS HUXLEY

You'll be surprised to find that performing acts of kindness, while being giving and grateful, will also increase your own happiness. The most fun thing about happiness is that you never know where you'll find it. One of the happiest moments of your week may be just around the corner, or on the next telephone call. It could be from a stranger you encounter at the store. There is happiness all around you, but you need to know how to look for it, and more importantly, how to act to receive it.

Happiness When You Least Expect It

Once, I even found happiness when I was shoveling snow. It was a very snowy evening and the forecast called for a total accumulation of approximately twelve inches of snow before morning. My nephew had flown into town that afternoon to take a high school entrance exam, and I had picked him up from the airport. The plan was for me to drive him to take the test the next morning. With the snow coming down pretty hard, I thought of the problems I might encounter in getting him to school on time.

My alarm went off at 5:30 am and I slowly dragged myself out of bed. Looking out my bedroom window, it was clear that the weather forecast was accurate. The fresh blanket of snow in my backyard was at least ten inches deep, and it was still snowing. I got dressed quickly, because I'd have to either begin shoveling the snow to get my vehicle out of the driveway, or fire up the snow blower at 6 am. Being the conscientious person I'd like to be at all times, I wondered if I might be waking up my neighbors on a snowy Saturday morning if I used the snow blower. The options weren't good and shoveling the snow would take at least an hour. My wife was already cooking breakfast for my nephew, ensuring that he took his test on a full stomach. I asked my wife what she thought and she gave me great advice: "Use the snow blower."

If you've never cleared a long driveway with twelve inches of snow, you've missed quite an experience. It's certainly better using a snow blower, rather than shoveling the entire driveway as I've done in the past, but it still takes work. Nonetheless, thirty minutes later, I had finished the driveway with the help of my snow blower. The sidewalk in front of my house had already been plowed by my next-door neighbor's son. Ron, routinely and without fanfare or pay, plowed much of our block with his small riding tractor. By 6:30 am, my nephew and I were off in the snowstorm to get him to his destination by 7:15 am. I didn't finish removing the snow from my walkway, from the sidewalk to the stairs, or from the sidewalk to the street. So I figured that I'd finish the snow removal when I got back home. The snow was continuing to fall, so I knew I'd have to remove more snow later in the day anyway.

Upon successfully getting my nephew to the school, I came back home with a mission to finish the snow removal job I started over an hour and a half earlier. I cleared the snow from around my house and also from my neighbor's walkway. While my neighbor had a snow plow, his snow blower wasn't working and the snow plow was too large to do his walkway. I enjoyed clearing the snow from both my driveway and the walkways for both of my next-door neighbors. There's nothing like a fresh snow fall with all the trees and houses covered in a fresh blanket of snow. At the time, I felt thankful that I was so blessed to enjoy the snow and the majesty of the fresh fallen snow at 7:45 am on a cold, snowy Saturday morning. I didn't want to go in the house, but my T-shirt was pretty wet from my sweating, and my dog and I were starting to get cold. As I put the snow blower in the garage, I glanced across the street and thought I saw someone standing with a shovel.

"Help …!"

Were my ears deceiving me or did I hear someone from across the street yelling for help? I was pretty sure that it must have been something else, since Rosalyn (my neighbor from across the street) often enjoyed shoveling her snow, and whoever I saw across the street didn't appear to be in any distress. I continued to put up the snow blower and was entering my back door when I had a second thought, "What if someone really needed help and I was going in the house anyway?" Sure, I was hot and tired at this point, but I thought it would be better to go check it out anyway.

As I walked back to the front of the house, across the street stood Rosalyn's seven-year-old son, Neal. Neal was standing in twelve inches of snow with a shovel. "Would you like a little help with the snow?" I asked in a voice much more pleasant than I was feeling at the time. Neal's cheeks were already turning red. He gave me the biggest smile and slowly said, "Yes, I need help."

"No problem," was my response, "and by the way, thanks for asking for help. Many people don't like asking for help, even when they need it."

Neal's smile lit up his face again. "Well, I really need help," he replied.

I couldn't help but laugh as I trudged across the street, back to my garage and pulled out the still-warm snow blower. No use in just doing the walkway, so I began with my neighbor's driveway.

"Then what can I do?" Neal wanted to know.

"Well, you can begin on your stairs, or shovel around the car," I told him.

Suddenly, my next-door neighbor drove up. Dean is a senior citizen and his son plows the sidewalks with the tractor. "Thanks so much for doing my walkway," Dean shouted to me over the sound of my continuously loud snow blower.

"Oh, my pleasure," I hollered back.

At that moment, Dean got out of his car with his shovel and walked toward my stairs. As many of you may know, snow blowers are good for many things, but it takes a shovel to remove the snow off the stairs. Besides, I wanted to leave the stairs for my son, who was still sleeping.

"Dean, you don't have to shovel my stairs," I screamed from across the street as I turned off the snow blower for a moment. "Besides I was leaving the stairs for my son."

"I want to do it," was Dean's reply.

Once again, I smiled and fired up the snow blower.

While finishing up the sidewalk of my neighbor across the street, I looked back at my house, where Neal had crossed the street and had joined Dean in shoveling my stairs. Apparently Neal liked the notion of helping Dean shovel my stairs, since he didn't have much to do at his own house.

Wow, I thought, this is a great. While I was removing the snow from in front of one neighbor's home, Dean and Neal were shoveling my stairs. No one had done anything with the thought of getting something in return. We were all just being good neighbors. What a great feeling! What a blessing!

In the couple of hours that it took for my snow removal escapade, I had experienced giving, kindness and being thankful. And, to think, that I would have missed it all if I had just gone in the house as I planned. As I looked across the street to see my neighbors finishing the snow removal from my stairs, I couldn't have been happier.

Let Happiness Find You

As stated in the Declaration of Independence, one of the rights of U.S. citizens is "the pursuit of happiness." More often, you pursue happiness, but sometimes happiness pursues you and you don't even know it.

> "All people act for what they think will make them happy."
> — Aristotle

Are you too busy in your pursuit of happiness to let happiness find you? Isn't the pursuit of happiness why you do most of the things you do? And what do you think will make you happy?

Your overall happiness and that of your child is not truly about your pursuit, but about *your* activities. Regardless of how you define happiness, if you increase the activities associated with being thankful, giving, and being kind, both you and your children will be much happier. You can make yours a happier home.

Take This with You:

- *Giving, thanks and kindness will increase your happiness.*
- *It's not about you.*
- *Your children are watching.*

And Remember:

- *Take a minute to reflect on the good stuff that is happening in your life—and everyone has some good stuff.*
- *Do something good for someone and expect nothing in return.*
- *Increase your activities associated with being thankful, kind, and giving.*

9
Spirituality

S tudies show that 95 percent of all parents believe in God. Income level doesn't matter. Neither does marital status or educational level.

A belief in God is something that can provide both you and your child with a foundation for life. Spirituality can give you a basis to make sound decisions, understand right from wrong, and provide a moral compass. With 95 percent of all parents believing in God, it doesn't seem that we should have the issues with morality that we have today. But yet we do.

Sometimes in life, things will go wrong and things will happen that you won't like. Somewhere, I read that "death is the price for living." You will probably experience the death of a loved one in life. When life's journey brings about the trials and tribulations that you and your child will experience, you'll need your faith to see you through. You'll need prayer and a faith that will keep you uplifted when things go wrong. Faith will keep you up when others all around you are down. You can be the positive energy that generates excitement in others.

spir-it   1: *that which constitutes one's unseen, intangible being*
                 2: *the essential and activating principle of a person*

Spirituality Helps Build Core Values

We live in a culture of instant gratification. Instant gratification means almost everyone is looking for a short-cut. While the biblical truth, "You reap what you sow," had meaning to a previous generation, it means little to many young people today. This is the age of BET, VH-1 and MTV. Parents must deal with music lyrics that often degrade women, praise sex at virtually any age, and glorify shootings and killings. If your child is getting their values from music, music videos, television and video games, then you will have a child with troublesome values.

These values will be troublesome for your child unless you've instilled other values. Spirituality can provide you with the core values and the boundaries that will make raising your child much easier. Boundaries are important in children, and there seem to be few public boundaries left.

When looking into high schools for my son, one of the schools provided me with an insight into different types of boundaries. In describing the difference between a few schools, the administrator stated that at one school, the guard rails (boundaries) were out here, with his arms extended and his hands six feet apart. At another school, the guard rails were about five feet apart. And at his school, the guard rails were three feet apart. I like that analogy when it comes to raising children.

A child's growth and education are like a road, and you are responsible for putting up the guard rails of life. Sometimes, the best guardrails in the world won't prevent a child from crashing or going over the guardrails and down the cliff. You have a duty to put up the best guardrails for your child, and spirituality can be your construction manager.

> *"One generation plants the trees and another gets the shade."*
> —OLD CHINESE PROVERB

Raising children today is much tougher than it was ten or twenty years ago. Our culture today has very few boundaries. Commonly accepted moral boundaries that existed not long ago have disappeared. Raising children with those boundaries in place was a much easier job then than it is today. Instilling spirituality and a belief in God in your children will give them a solid foundation for life long after you're gone.

While I'm a Christian, I won't suggest that my beliefs are right and those that practice another religion are wrong. The key for everyone isn't to be a good Christian, but to believe in God and to teach your children the law of God. Most religions have a common theme about integrity, character, justice and practical issues of life. There are many life lessons to be gained through spirituality, and you have the responsibility to train your children with wisdom from God.

"It Begins with You"

Let's remember that "it begins with you." It does no good to teach children good judgment when you don't practice good judgment yourself. It's hard for parents to be one thing and to expect their children to be something else.

Unlike today, in the past, many black children were raised in religious homes, and sometimes we didn't even know it. I was raised in what I thought was a normal type of household. My father worked as a truant officer, a role that doesn't exist in many school districts today. Just in case you're not sure, a truant officer was a position associated with the Board of Education to make sure that children attended school. If you didn't show up in school, a truant officer would either come by your house, or call your house to see why you hadn't made it to school. With a father as a truant officer, I can tell you that playing hooky from school was a thought that never entered my tender, feeble mind.

We ate breakfast together in the mornings and always sat around the dinner table together in the evenings. My father said the blessing at the dinner table and everyone else at the table had to say a Bible verse. Of course, my favorite Bible verse was the shortest one in the bible, "Jesus wept." My sister enjoyed torturing us with long verses that made it that much longer before we could eat. And on Sundays, we went to church. There wasn't a discussion about wanting to go to church or feeling like going to church, we all went to church or at least Sunday school.

My mother was raised in a religious, single-parent household and often spoke at various churches as a Woman's Day speaker. When my mother spoke at a church, you could bet that her husband and all of her children would be in attendance. While my mother didn't get a college diploma, she attended many college classes after high school and was introduced to my father (thanks Aunt Minnie) at a seminar on public speaking in 1943. My parents were married in 1946, and never considered raising their children in anything other than a Christian household.

While my father was raised as a Roman Catholic and my mother as a Baptist, in their eyes a good Christian was still a good Christian. My mother often listened to religious music and enjoyed watching a few of the TV ministers on Sunday mornings. But our house wasn't what you would think of as a religious household, or at least not what I thought of as a religious household. My parents were of the school that you could be a good Christian and still have fun. You could be a good Christian and enjoy an occasional adult beverage. You could be a good Christian and play cards. You could be a good Christian and dance. You could be a good Christian and party! They even had a host of other married friends who formed a couples club that got together every month at each other's house to have conversation and to party. Our house was based on religious beliefs, but we also had big fun.

A Life Based on Spirituality and the Golden Rule

One day, a friend of mine came over to my house and my mother had on some gospel music. My friend knew I regularly went to church and as soon as we got outside he stated, "I didn't know you lived in a religious house."

"What do you mean?" I replied.

"Well, you like to have fun, dance, go to parties and other good stuff," he said. "Your parents seem pretty cool, so I was surprised that you live in such a religious house."

"I never thought of it as living in a religious house," I told him.

"Well, you do," I was informed.

You know, I think he was right. My parents based our life-style on spirituality and religious beliefs. The Golden Rule was the rule in our home, and it became the basis for how I treat everyone. Some of the spiritual teachings that I learned from my parents included:

- Watch what you say. Words have power.
- Love thy neighbor.
- The value of hard work.
- Worship.
- Obey your parents.
- Chose your friends wisely.
- Protect your mind.
- Love God.

With spirituality as a basis for your boundaries, you can make a dramatic difference in your children and in how they see the world. And today more than ever before, your child needs boundaries. Spirituality can provide just what both you and your child need. Our culture today would have you think that your net worth is how you determine your self-worth. Nothing could be further from the truth. Spirituality can teach your child that life has value, regardless of your material possessions.

"Keep Hope Alive"

Everyone would like to live a long, healthy and happy life. Putting spirituality in your child's life can provide the foundation they need and help you set the boundaries. Spirituality can provide hope where no hope is apparent. Is it just me, or does it seem that many children seemingly have little or no hope? If you looked into their lives further, I bet you'd find that these same kids have little spirituality in their lives.

> *"Train up a child in the way he should go: and when he is old, he will not depart from it."*
> — *Proverbs 22:6*

Hope is critical in life, and one of my favorite lines I first heard decades ago from the Rev. Jesse Jackson is, "Keep hope alive." You must have hope and your child must have hope. Spirituality can always provide you with hope. You must keep hope alive in your child. Where there is no hope, the people will perish. The same is true for you and your child.

Bad Examples Abound

Just the other day, I went to a mall to purchase a gift for my teenage nephew. Living in a big city, the malls often cater to the young urban crowd. Urban used to be a code word for black, but the hip-hop generation and urban clothes now include a multitude of young white youth, too. You can find stores in malls all across America and throughout many countries in Europe with urban clothes, even in the whitest of communities.

Strolling into a store that catered to young adults, the first noticeable difference was that the music was blasting! The music was way too loud for me, but this wasn't the first time I had experienced loud music in a store. But one thing was very different; the music that was ripping my ear drums apart was not only loud, it was also X-rated. Yes, loud, X-rated, hip-hop or rap music blasted throughout a store in a mall in America. How disgusting! I asked the young lady behind the counter if she could change the music because I thought it was offensive and she said, "No problem." I found out that whoever was working the store could play the music they wanted. I quickly left the store without buying a thing.

A society with strong values based on spirituality would never let a store playing X-rated music exist in a mall or anywhere else. Years ago, a store blasting foul-mouthed music would have been run out of the mall and couldn't possibly exist. Today, this type of store is thriving throughout America.

Our society today lets these kinds of stores exist because we as consumers don't demand that they stop such outlandish behavior. Some businesses and many people will do almost anything for money. You must teach your child the difference between right and wrong, and as consumers, parents should not support such establishments. If you're rooted in spirituality, you have a foundation to stand up for what you know is right, and your child will as well.

Rock Solid—The Foundation of Spirituality

Some things will change, but the foundations of spirituality are rock solid, and this is one of those areas where *you* won't have to change. You may have to modify a curfew or change some rules as your child gets older, but the foundation provided by spirituality will not change. And both you and your child will reap the benefits for the rest of your lives.

Spirituality can also provide both you and your child with the most powerful tool you'll ever possess, the power to change how you think and the power to train your mind. It includes training both your heart and your mind. Your mind is the most powerful thing you possess, and spirituality can help you train your mind.

Two Ways to See Life

There are at least two ways to see almost every situation, and it may take a change in thinking to get you to see the positive side of things. You could look at it as the positive side versus the negative side, or good versus evil, or the choice to do the right thing or the wrong thing. The famous comedian Flip Wilson had a hilarious routine about not doing the right thing that he called "The Devil Made Me Do It." It was a great routine. Many people look to blame anyone but themselves for their issues, even the devil. Spirituality can guide you to "do the right thing."

When my children were younger, I often used a *Star Wars* analogy. A part of good communication is to know your audience, and since most children were familiar with the *Star Wars* saga, it seemed to work well. As you may know, *Star Wars* has been extremely popular and one of the interesting aspects of the series is the common themes between spirituality and "The Force." Luke Skywalker and Obi-Wan Kenobi represent those that use The Force for good, while Darth Vader and company utilize the dark side of The Force for evil.

The way you look at any situation can be viewed in much the same manner. Look at the glass as half-full, rather than half-empty. Look at things that happen in your life as an opportunity. The old saying that "Every cloud has a silver lining" is quite true; it just depends on how you see things. Spirituality can change how you see *everything*.

The dark side is very powerful, and you'll be doing a disservice to your children if you don't equip them with spirituality to help them in life's journey to battle the dark side. The dark side will enter your life in many forms. Sometimes, it's another person and how he or she treats you, or in its strongest form, as a part of your innermost thoughts. Spirituality is the best defense.

When Hard Times Come

When life's hardships hit your child, as they eventually will, hopefully you will have prepared your child for life's journey by instilling the power of God and faith. It won't be a matter of if the hardships will hit, it's only a matter of when.

As a parent, you play a pivotal role when it comes to spirituality and your child. You must teach your child the importance of spirituality, for children are taught to be what they become.

Not long ago, I heard a great sermon by Rev. Marshall Hatch of the New Mount Pilgrim Baptist Church in Chicago, Illinois. The essence of the sermon was that for parents to make a change, they needed to plant a new seed. Parents can determine what they plant, where they plant, and when they plant. Then they must claim responsibility for their own seeds. They can plant a new seed in their own heart.

The word of God is a new seed. The word of God can be a new seed that you can use to make you think differently and behave differently. 95 percent of parents believe in God. Income level doesn't matter. Neither does marital status or educational level. So use God. For the word of God is the most powerful ally you will ever have.

Take This with You:

- *A belief in God can serve as the best foundation.*
- *Spirituality will help you set boundaries and structure.*
- *Set the moral values in your home.*

And Remember:

- *Attend a place of worship. For me it's a church. For you, it may be a mosque, a temple or another type of service. The key is to go!*
- *Take your child with you.*
- *Pray.*

10
The Most Important Years

By the age of three, your child will have developed at least 70 percent of his or her brain cells. Experts agree that the most critical time in the development of a child will be between birth and three years old. It doesn't take much money to provide a stimulating environment for a young child, but it does take time and commitment. The first five years of your child's life are critical to their development. Those years might be critical years during development, but if your child is older, then those critical years are history. However, there are still things you can do.

From here on, the most important years in your child's life are the next years. That's right, the next years can still make the difference in your child. Child development is great, and if you have a newborn or a toddler, you can maximize crucial lessons in raising your child. But what if you don't?

Children come in all ages and shapes, and your children are where they are today. You can't change the past, but you can learn from it and strive to get better. So can you *still* make a difference? Absolutely!

It Begins with You

Since you still have the ability to change your own behaviors and attitude, you can still positively influence your child. And we're right back where we started: It begins with you. So what goals would *you* like to accomplish with your child in the next year? Improve school grades, increase reading, provide a better environment, implement house rules, or manage expectations? The goals you put in place should be based on your children and their ages. There is no one answer for every child, so *you* will have to determine the goals. Determine your goals, write them down and review them every month.

In the next year, you can increase your children's reading and enhance their educational experience. Turn off the television for an hour a day and replace it with family reading time is one suggestion. Could you put guidelines in place so your child is better prepared for school by enforcing a time for bed and a time to rise? What if you set daily limits for television and video games? This could get good!

What if, in the next year, *you* decide to choose your attitude every day and spend more time with your child? What if you raised *your* expectations of your child and provided an environment that supports your expectations? Might you get more involved in your child's school and get to know his or her teachers?

Sitting at home *reading* rather than watching Trisha Goddard or Maury Povich might influence your children. What if you ate dinner with your children and asked, "What was different in school today?" Bet you find out a few things you didn't know. But you gotta ask questions, and you gotta take time to listen to the answers.

What if you went to church and took your son or daughter? Think it might make a difference? What if you pray? Pray and thank God for waking up this morning, pray for your children, and pray for a sound mind that allows you to make choices. What if you laugh a little more every day and play with your children? That could really be fun; laughing usually is. What if you set personal goals and take actionable steps to achieve them?

Don't Wait, Start Now!

The most important time is now, and the most important years are the next ones. In the next year, you can change your life and the life of a child. Now is the time to start.

So with what goal would you like to start?

My opinion is that you should write down a goal right now (don't wait), and start working toward this goal each and every day. Once you achieve this goal, celebrate, then go on to the next one, and the next one. Yes, it may be hard. But achieving your goals will be well worth the effort. And if some days you have a hard time staying on task and start to fall back into bad habits, remind yourself of this one important fact:

Your child's life depends on you setting a path for success. This should provide you with all the motivation you will ever need.

Take this with You:

- *What you do next is what matters most.*
- *You are either setting your children up for success, or setting them up for failure.*
- *Your actions are critical.*

And Remember:

- *Make your goals actionable.*
- *Everyone is accountable for their actions.*
- *Laugh a little, cry a little, and love a lot.*

Appendix A

Suggested Reading

Raising Black Children, by James Comer and Alvin Poussaint
Playful Parenting, by Lawrence Cohen
The 7 Habits of Highly Effective People, by Stephen Covey
The Black Parenting Book, by Allison Abner, Linda Villarosa and
    Anne Beal
The Ultimate Parenting Map to Money Smart Kids, by Linda Leitz

Appendix B

It Begins with You

Take This with You:

- *Have a vision and write it down.*
- *Be consistent and stay determined.*
- *You are the answer.*

And Remember:

- *Write down your goals.*
- *Make a plan.*
- *Take action.*

The Environment

Take This with You:

- *Control your surroundings.*
- *Manage the monitors in your home.*
- *Influence your child more than anyone else.*

And Remember:

- *Set daily limits for TV, video games and the Internet.*
- *Provide balance by supporting activities such as reading, puzzles and board games.*
- *Be consistent and communicate.*

House Rules

Take This with You:

- *Children need guidelines, so establish house rules.*
- *Communicate clearly.*
- *Everyone in the house must abide by the rules.*

And Remember:

- *As the parent, you determine the rules.*
- *Set up an educational support structure.*
- *Enforce your rules.*

Managing Expectations

Take This with You:

- *Set high expectations.*
- *Children want to please.*
- *Define success.*

And Remember:

- *Manage the expectations.*
- *Expect good things.*
- *Determine your child's habits.*

Attitude Is Everything

Take This with You:

- *Build an educational foundation.*
- *Confidence is an attitude.*
- *Focus on the positive.*

And Remember:

- *Involve your child in a preschool program.*
- *Use positive words.*
- *Choose your attitude.*

Reading

Take This with You:

- *Reading gives you the ability to continuously learn.*
- *Reading can give you hope.*
- *Reading is about you.*

And Remember:

- *Get your child a library card and use the library.*
- *Establish a family reading hour.*
- *Read every day*

Happiness

Take This with You:

- *Giving, thanks and kindness will increase your happiness.*
- *It's not about you.*
- *Your children are watching.*

And Remember:

- *Take a minute to reflect on the good stuff that is happening in your life—and everyone has some good stuff.*
- *Do something good for someone and expect nothing in return.*
- *Increase your activities associated with being thankful, kind, and giving.*

Spirituality

Take This with You:

- *A belief in God can serve as the best foundation.*
- *Spirituality will help you set boundaries and structure.*
- *Set the moral values in your home.*

And Remember:

- *Attend a place of worship. For me it's a church. For you, it may be a mosque, a temple or another type of service. The key is to go!*
- *Take your child with you.*
- *Pray.*

The Most Important Years

Take this with You:

- *What you do next is what matters most.*
- *You are either setting your child up for success, or setting them up for failure.*
- *Your actions are critical.*

And Remember:

- *Make your goals actionable.*
- *Everyone is accountable for their actions.*
- *Laugh a little, cry a little, and love a lot.*